BREATHING AGAIN

Finding Peace While Navigating
Faith Reconstruction

Kristen Neighbarger

©2024 by Kristen Neighbarger

Published by hope*books

2217 Matthews Township Pkwy

Suite D302

Matthews, NC 28105

www.hopebooks.com

hope*books is a division of hope*media

Printed in the United States of America

First paperback edition.

Paperback ISBN: 979-8-89185-078-1

Hardcover ISBN: 979-8-89185-079-8

Ebook ISBN: 979-8-89185-085-9

Library of Congress Number: 2024940269

hope*books
hopebooks.com

"I've always said that there's only one way to deconstruct, and that's your way! I love Kristen Neighbarger's personal, honest and thorough account of her own deconstruction because it helps the rest of us who are experiencing it feel normal. This is a natural, healthy, and necessary journey we call spiritual growth. If you want another angle on how deconstruction is done, read this book."

David Hayward, aka NakedPastor,
Author of *The Lasting Supper: Letters for Deconstruction*

"For anyone deconstructing and reconstructing their faith, *Breathing Again* will quite literally be a breath of fresh air. Writing gently with personal stories, Kristen validates her readers, gives them permission to be on their faith journey, and lets them know that they are not alone."

Christy Lynne Wood Author of *Religious Rebels: Seeking Jesus in the Awkward Middle Way*

"When it comes to the Christian faith, most of us face the realization that the foundational beliefs we've always assumed to be true are not as faultless as we once believed. By closely examining God's Word, Kristen guides her readers through the process of deconstructing faulty beliefs and building renewed foundations. This book is a breath of fresh air for anyone who has felt stifled by the rules of Christianity, hurt by the church, or disillusioned by faith."

Stacey Pardoe Author of *Lean Into Grace: Let God's Grace Heal Your Heart, Refresh Your Soul, and Set You Free*

"In *Breathing Again,* Kristen Neighbarger courageously shares her raw and relatable journey of faith deconstruction and reconstruction. With transparency, vulnerability, and insight, she guides readers through the often painful process of examining the difference between what's truly God-ordained and what's merely culture-driven. "Breathing Again" is a beautiful example of unraveling religious beliefs, church hurts, and spiritual trauma — and emerging on the other side with a renewed faith foundation."

Cortney Farmer
Co-Founder and Head Writer at The Soft Never

"*Breathing Again* is a must-read to help those who are healing from past church trauma. Hope and encouragement flow from the pages as Kristen shares her experiences, giving applicable steps to achieve healing while moving closer to God. This book brought multiple "me too" moments, encouraging me to pursue healing from those past hurts."

Brianna Barrett
Author and Photographer

TABLE OF CONTENTS

INTRODUCTION

We stood in the front yard and stared at the two-story house in front of us.

"It doesn't look that bad," I said to my dad, my normal three-part optimism overtaking my one-part realism. "I definitely see the potential here, and at this price, in this economy, in this school district! We'd be stupid not to jump on this right now before someone else does."

My dad's eyes narrowed a little as I rambled on, his tell-tale sign of mentally calculating all the details of a task I don't see or choose to ignore when the dreamer part of my brain takes over. I saw his hand come up to his chin and rest there for a minute as he tilted his head to the side, raising his eyes just a fraction, and I knew I was gaining at least a little bit of ground.

We walked around to the back of the house. I noted the original log cabin from the 1800s that sat by the pond on the backside of the property, another log structure with multiple additions that was functioning as a barn, a springhouse, another outbuilding, and two other garages.

"The back side of the house doesn't look so bad," I said with weary optimism.

"There is literally a tree growing on the roof, over there by that giant hole in the roof of the back porch," Dad responded.

"Well, yeah, but we'd need to rip that part off anyway," I said, losing a little more of my optimism.

"And that corner of the house is a solid 8 inches lower than that other corner," he continued as logic and realism attacked me head-on.

"I see that, " I said, "but the roof on the rest of the house looks great! And have you seen inside those windows? The house is full, and I'm sure there are countless treasures in there we can sell to make back the asking price before we even start on the renovations."

For the record, I was wrong. There were no treasures inside this house. What was inside this house was every DVD and VHS tape known to man. The previous owner had bought the inventory of a Blockbuster store that was closing and kept everything for himself. And milk jugs. Lots and lots of milk jugs. Oh, and everything else the previous owner had ever owned. If you've ever seen one of those shows about hoarders, this house and all of the outbuildings could have easily been the subject of one of them.

Looking back on this scene, I'm honestly not sure how I convinced my dad that buying this hoarder property was a good idea. I guess the price was right because buy it, we did. Looking back now, the adventure of renovating that hoarder house was one for the record books.

It took us a week just to clean the contents of the house out—not to demo the inside of the house, which would come later, but to simply clean all of the stuff out of the house. We spent days separating all the contents of the house into piles for Goodwill, the dump, and the scrapyard. I finally stopped counting how many trips we took to all three places. It was that bad.

When we finally rid the house of all the stuff in it, we had to face the demolition head-on. My dad and I are both stubborn visionaries. When we work together on these projects, we spend endless hours sitting on sawhorses in various parts of the house, staring at walls, measuring rooms, and conjecturing about all the possibilities. During this pre-demolition time, my dad, who has decades of construction and renovation experience compared to my few years, patiently shoots down my hair-brained and structurally impossible ideas. Inevitably, though, we end up arriving at a design that we both love or at least can agree we'll try to love before we start tearing out floors, ripping out walls, and, in this case, raising one corner of the house a solid 8 inches.

When we have a tentative plan in place, the demolition process can begin. This is one of my favorite parts of renovating. There is something so cathartic about pulling off plaster, tearing out walls, watching worn-out floors go on the trash pile, and stripping things bare. Part of the joy for me is watching as the old is removed to make way for the new. I know we have to rip it all out before we can rebuild it into something beautiful. Then, there's the other part, which is the satisfaction of walking outside at the end of the day and staring at the giant piles of rubble left over after the demolition.

There's also something about that point in the renovation process when we've torn everything out, and the house is nothing more than a skeleton of what it once was, some rooms nothing more than floor joists and studs. On the one hand, it feels so empty, but on the other hand, untapped potential and promise are waiting for us. I think that's one of the most unforgettable moments of a renovation project– that point in time when all the demolition is done, the house is eerily quiet, and the excitement of what's coming is buzzing in the air.

That's also the point in the renovation journey where the temptation to throw in the towel and walk away is at its highest. While you're exhilarated by the possibilities ahead, you're also exhausted by all the work you've already done. It's that moment where every renovator stops and weighs the return on investment to determine if they are better off selling now or finishing the project. We could have stopped our renovations right there, sold that house, and walked away from it with probably triple our investment in our pockets. We could have easily made this reconstruction process someone else's project.

But where is the joy in that?

While I love demolition and staring at a house that has been stripped to its skeleton, those feelings don't compare to what it feels like to stand in the yard and look at it on the day it gets listed with the realtor – when the reconstruction is complete, the house is whole, and the property itself looks like nothing short of a miracle.

There are days leading up to that moment when it feels like we'll never get there. There are weeks – even months – where it feels like we are just all holding our breaths, praying we'll make it across the finish line as we face issues, unseen problems, and challenges we weren't expecting. Despite those daunting moments, we always keep on keeping on. Sometimes that means running to Home Depot three times in one day, or throwing in the towel and going to Chipotle for lunch, or taking a much-needed Saturday off.

On the day the sales contract is signed, and then when it's closed and sold, we look back with a myriad of emotions–some sadness, some anger, some frustration, but ultimately joy and pride at what we accomplished, relieved that we didn't just sell it after we tore everything out.

My experience renovating a house with my dad eerily parallels my experience with my faith deconstruction and reconstruction journey. I approached deconstructing my faith similarly to how I approached the demolition of the hoarder house–I tore it apart until nothing was left but a few joists and studs.

I was left with two things: a giant pile of rubble and a skeleton of what once had been. And I felt like I was holding my breath the entire time I sorted through the rubble and reconstructed my house.

Admittedly, there were times when I just wanted to throw in the towel and quit, when I felt like I couldn't continue to work through that giant pile of rubble to determine what was worth keeping and what needed to be burnt and destroyed. There were also times, though, when I stood in front of that house that was nothing more than a skeleton and thought one match was all it would take to burn it all to the ground, and I had an entire match-book and a lighter at my disposal.

Just like my dad and I didn't have a guidebook or fancy blue-prints to guide us toward the reconstruction of the hoarder house, I didn't have a blueprint or even a guide to lead me through my faith reconstruction.

During the renovation, some days, we would walk away from the job site feeling like we accomplished greatness and other days, we would walk away feeling like we had taken two steps forward and five steps backward. That's the same way I felt as I worked on reconstructing my faith. Some days, I felt like I could see and final-ly cross the finish line, and other days, I wondered if the finish line even existed. Just like when we renovated the hoarder house, as soon as one aspect of my faith reconstruction was complete, it was right on to the next. Finally, I came to a place where I could take a few steps away from the project and see all the progress I'd made and know I'd crossed at least a milestone, if not the finish line.

Even though there were times when I was sorting through the rubble that I wondered if I would be able to build something worthwhile from the ransacked debris and fragile-looking skeleton, I persevered. Through my perseverance, I experienced every emotion under the sun. I was angry at the theology I had been taught, sad at the community I lost, hurt by the damage that such terrible theology inflicted on me, and anxious that all the work I was doing might possibly be for nothing.

As I became more comfortable with the reconstruction process, though, I realized I was experiencing a new set of emotions. I experienced joy in this freedom for the first time. I was overwhelmed as I began to understand unconditional love and God's intention for grace. I was content with who God created me to uniquely be. I was at peace with the fact that I didn't have all the answers and that I might never have them.

For the majority of my life, I had been holding my breath, praying that I was somehow going to be good enough – that I was performing enough, making good enough choices, earning enough of God's love, doing enough to please God, serving enough, loving enough, being selfless enough. Enough. Enough. Enough.

The weight of "enough" kept me from breathing freely in peace and truth. My journey through deconstruction and reconstruction allowed me to recognize that I am a survivor of spiritual abuse, church hurt, and religious trauma. Once I understood and accepted that, I was able to pursue healing that allowed me to finally breathe in peace, truth, and freedom as I navigated my faith reconstruction journey.

That's my prayer and my hope for you as you walk with me through my journey and work through your own reconstruction journey – that today is the first day of freeing yourself from the weight that is holding you down and keeping you from breathing deeply and fully in your healing, your peace, your truth, and your freedom.

When I was a little girl, I watched the dandelions in our yard change from their dense, ugly, yellow flowers to nothing more than these light, fuzzy fronds. They would blow away with one short exhale of breath. As you work through the dense, ugly truth of your own survival of spiritual abuse, church hurt, and/or religious trauma, I pray those memories and that damage become as light as those dead, fluffy dandelion fronds you can blow away with one single breath.

I pray that today is the first day you can take enough of a breath to watch as the dead blow away and make room for new life.

1

BREATHING DEEPLY:
GIVING YOURSELF PERMISSION
TO BREATHE AGAIN

It was a Sunday morning like any other. I was sitting in my self-assigned seat in the next-to-last row in the church building that looked more like an abandoned warehouse than a sanctuary. The lights were dimmed, the worship was complete, and the band was transitioning to the pensive music that would play behind the individual sharing their thoughts and then praying for communion.

I was anxious – more anxious than I would have been if I were the one delivering those words and that prayer. I watched from my seat in the back as my 17-year-old daughter, Kate, waited at the bottom of the steps on stage left.

Even though she spent nine years of her life dancing on stages in front of audiences full of hundreds of people, this was the first time she had dared to take the mic, use her voice, and speak to a church. I was used to being in that spot in the middle of the stage, lights blinding me, all eyes on me, camera recording.

She wasn't.

Had I prepared her?

Did I let her practice enough?

Would she enunciate?

Would people listen?

All those panicky mom thoughts raced through my brain simultaneously, not allowing me to really process any one of them completely. I watched as she situated herself in the center of the stage, opened her phone to the app where she had written out her thoughts, and I listened as she spoke.

She had just returned from a mission trip to Pittsburgh, and she told of how they went to Wal-Mart and split into groups, each one tasked with picking out a different part of the meal they would pass out – instructed to only get food they would eat themselves or food that was better than what their parents bought them at home.

After the shopping was complete, they packed sack lunches, loaded coolers with ice water, and headed to one of the tent cities in downtown Pittsburgh. As they passed out sack lunches, they talked to these folks. They treated them as the humans they truly are. They made room at their table for the least of these.

I listened as she made the connection between her own experiences in Pittsburgh and Jesus's table, and as she talked about Jesus spending his last supper with Judas, who would betray Him, and Peter, who would deny Him. She talked about the fact that our tables need to look more like Jesus's table, and how our tables should be open to everyone–especially the least of these. I listened as she made the connection to the fact that we never know when we might find ourselves in the position of the least of these – as addicts, homeless, betrayers, or deniers.

I listened, and I wept.

It wasn't just the fact that my kid was on the stage speaking so honestly, humbly, and frankly, although that was definitely part of it. It was the fact that I was sitting in a church on a Sunday morning, listening to a 17-year-old girl speak from the stage and pray for communion. That never would have happened in my church growing up. Sadly, it still wouldn't happen in many churches around the country today – or down the road, or even next door in so many cases.

The weight of that sat heavily on my chest– had been sitting heavily on my chest for decades, honestly. As I watched Kate and listened to her speak again, I felt like I could breathe again, or, in some ways, even breathe for the first time. It was palpable.

HOME AT LAST

On the scale of stubbornness and thick-headedness, I'm admittedly up there – not quite a ten but pretty close. I've come to accept the fact that God knows this flaw of mine and consequently understands I'm not a good example of "blind faith." I have more of a "set the fleece out three or four times before it sinks in" kind of faith.

This Sunday was no exception.

After Kate stood and proudly delivered her communion thoughts and prayer, I noticed it wasn't just one of our three pastors heading to the stage. Instead, it was one of our pastors, Jason, and his wife, Anne. As they took the stage, they immediately pulled up a couple of stools, and each grabbed their mics. I felt the smile spread across my face as they preached together. I struggled to identify each of the emotions I was feeling at that moment but settled on pride, peace, healing, and acceptance.

Again, more of that weight of church hurt, spiritual abuse, and faulty theology that I had been carrying around for decades continued to lift off my shoulders in that warehouse on that ordinary Sunday.

Home.

I knew I was home.

Even though I had attended this church, been active in this church, worshiped, and served in this church for years, this was the moment when I finally felt the weight of those years of church hurt and spiritual abuse from my adolescence and early adulthood begin to break free.

6TH GRADE PHARISEE

So much of my church hurt and trauma stemmed from the marginalizing theology I was taught related to women – in the church, at home, and in marriage. When I was in 6th grade, my best friend was Embrey. Our school district had four elementary schools that fed into our junior high and high school. It was a rural school district with little transiency. Most of the students I left sixth grade with were the same students I started Kindergarten with.

It was a small school district, so we only had one class of each grade level at each elementary school. When we had a new student, it was a big deal. A really big deal.

Embrey was one of those rare students who switched elementary schools in fifth grade, igniting the full fire of every one of my classmates' attention. I don't know exactly how it came to be that we became friends, but by the time we were in sixth grade, we were scheduling sleepovers and spending as much time together as we could. That was no small feat for us. As I mentioned, we were in a rural school district in Ohio, and it was the 80s. We went to town once a week – on Friday nights – to get groceries for the week, and if we didn't get it then, it had to wait until the next week.

I was never allowed to stay at Embrey's house on Saturday nights because we went to church on Sunday mornings, but I was allowed to have her spend the night with me on Saturday nights so that she could go to church with us on Sunday mornings.

I don't remember what happened the first time Embrey went to church with me, but I'll never forget the fallout from that morning. It was an innocent conversation on her part. While we had talked about church in the past, I didn't know the particulars of her church experience. I had no way of knowing that her pastor was a woman or that she attended a Presbyterian church—both things that would exclude her from heaven and send her straight to hell, according to the theology of my church.

Because of my religious brainwashing, I thought it was my job to convert her so she would go to heaven. I laid out for her all the perfectly logical and biblically-based reasons why she was going to hell with all the authority of an indoctrinated tween. I'm sure I pulled no punches and went straight for the jugular because that's who I was in those years.

I told her how women were not allowed to be preachers or even teach men because the Bible clearly stated that there was a hierarchy that placed God at the top, men next, women after, and finally, children. I explained that because she had not been fully immersed in the waters of Christian baptism, she was, sadly, unsaved, and I really didn't want her to burn in hell. I explained that all these denominations were created by man to teach their own ideas instead of the Bible and that my church was the only true church that followed exactly what the Bible said.

In my ignorance and Pharisaical attitude, I insulted and degraded everything she knew to be true and everything she knew to be good. I've made my fair share of mistakes in my life, but every time I think about this interaction, about the Pharisee that I was in this situation, about the judgment I heaped upon this innocent friend of mine, and the fallout from it, I'm ashamed, embarrassed, and beyond remorseful.

I put her on our prayer list in my Sunday School class. Seriously. I put my best friend, my Jesus-loving best friend, on the prayer list at my church because I was scared for her salvation because she went to a Presbyterian church with a female pastor.

Good grief. I can't make this stuff up.

And here's the thing that's even more disturbing as I think back on it:

- No one told me any different.
- No one laughed when I talked about it in my Sunday School class.
- No one told me how wrong I was.
- No one batted an eyelash.

Why?

Because they believed it, too. These adults weren't concerned that I was praying for this girl's salvation because of where she went to church. They encouraged it. As I think about it now as an adult, it makes me sick.

As our sixth-grade year went on, Embrey and I had many arguments about church and women's roles in the church. I wish I could say they were discussions, but I hadn't been taught to listen and discuss; I had been taught by the church to cherry-pick and argue. Eventually, this 12-year-old, who was so much wiser than me, wrote me a note and put it in my Bible, where it stayed for years and years.

Thoughtfully and with exceptional wisdom, Embrey had written me a note where she lovingly explained the women who ministered with Jesus and the Scriptures discussing spiritual gifts – Scriptures that didn't delineate between men and women. She wrote from her heart about the different female pastors she knew who were called to ministry, who she knew loved God, and who she knew were heeding their individual calling from God – despite their gender.

She lovingly asked me how I could hold these beliefs, being the strong female I was. How could I be so smart and articulate and believe that girls could do everything boys could do if I believed God discriminated against women in this way?

I wish I could tell you this note changed my life, that it made me begin to question my church's teaching and theology, and that I left in a fury, burning all those beliefs to the ground. I didn't. I still thought she was wrong because I was so brainwashed I was completely unable to see the validity of her points and only responded with the arguments I had been taught.

I had been trained to believe a very specific thing about God's view of women in the church, but even more depressing to me, I had been instructed on exactly what Scripture passages to use and what arguments to give when faced with this specific brand of heretics.

I hate that.

I hate looking back and knowing this was who I was at 12 years old, how judgmental and hateful I was – all in "the name of Jesus." Embrey and I never talked about it again. I continued to pray for her salvation. She never went to church with me again. When junior high hit, we went our separate ways and found different friends.

But I kept that note in my Bible.

Something about her words and her love piqued something in my subconscious that I wouldn't be able to truly put my finger on until years later. Sitting in that service in that warehouse on that Sunday morning, listening to two women preach God-given words to an entire faith community, stirred my memories again. It made me think of that note, of the impassioned Pharisee I was, and how wrong I was. It was an unavoidable clash of my past and present that needed to happen.

I don't know where Embrey is today. I haven't seen her since we graduated high school in 1997. If I ran into her on the street, at a football game, or even in the grocery store, the first thing I would do would be apologize to her and tell her how wrong I was and how right she was. I would thank her for the wisdom she wielded at 12 and the compassion she had for this spiteful, judgmental Pharisee. I would tell her how I carried her note around in my Bible for years – through moves, marriages, motherhood, divorces, deaths, tragedy, trauma, deconstruction, and reconstruction.

The process of deconstruction and reconstruction is like that, isn't it? It hits you in all the feels, it cracks open all the wounds, and it makes you see yourself and the world so very differently. It requires you to completely disassemble the set of beliefs you've held, to agonize over the rubble, and then make a choice: to rebuild or to walk away. So often, for so many people, the choice to rebuild is just too painful because the damage has been too much. But, for others, standing there looking at the wreckage of their faith traditions sparks something: a desire to clean up, a desire to put it back together again but with renovations, revisions, and remodeling. That's what reconstruction is all about—taking the rubble and rebuilding it into something true, beautiful, and your own.

I hope that's why you're here today – because you've already done the hard work of deconstruction, and now you find yourself asking, "What now?"

If you're like me at all, then you know you aren't the same person that you were before deconstructing, but you're still trying to figure out who you are post-deconstruction. I'm guessing you probably find yourself standing back, looking at all the ruin that's left over from your deconstructing. You're trying to figure out how to put it back together again. Or, maybe you're looking at that pile of rubble, and you know you need to start by sorting it out. You have to meticulously go through it to determine what's trash and what's salvageable. And then, after you've done the difficult job of sorting through it, you have to figure out how to rebuild–what to reuse, what to upcycle, and what to completely build from scratch.

Goodness. This is a process.

If you're feeling a little lost, a little like your life and beliefs exist somewhere in the margins, you're frequently misunderstood, and your old church friends have labeled you a bit of a misfit – whether to your face or behind your back – I see you. I'm here for you, and I'm here for this. For the long haul. For as long as it takes you to be able to sit in that place of peace and breathe again for the first time in what probably feels like forever.

I'm committed to helping you navigate this journey so you can breathe freely in a community where you feel the weight of church hurt, spiritual abuse, toxic theology, and maybe even deconstruction lifting off of your shoulders.

We're going to get through this together. We're going to work through this reconstruction together. It's probably going to be painful. It's probably going to stretch you. It's probably going to involve some ugly crying. But we will persist and persevere together – the misfits, the marginalized, and the misunderstood.

HOPE FOR TOMORROW

Standing over that pile of rubble that's left over from your deconstruction can feel daunting and completely overwhelming. I remember feeling like I had no idea where to even start as I began attempting to rebuild and reconstruct. One of the biggest struggles I had was attempting to see theology and spirituality with clear eyes instead of through the religious lens I had been raised in. I felt like I had spent my entire life without the ability to focus on what was around me; I could only see what the church had placed directly in front of me.

My mom struggles with this same issue with her literal eyesight. On June 5, 2009, my parents were out on a country ride on their motorcycle. They were in a small town in rural Ohio when a car pulled out in front of them, striking the Harley my dad had been driving for years, and then speeding away through a shopping center parking lot – never stopping or even braking to see if my parents were okay.

While they both were injured, my mom's injuries were much more extensive. One of her injuries was a traumatic brain injury (TBI). Although my mom now has a myriad of issues relating to her cognitive and language processing, she has no peripheral vision. None. She has to turn her head completely to the side to see if something is coming at her.

I didn't even realize how bad this was until one morning when we passed each other walking on the road. My mom was finishing up her walk and heading right for me, except she wasn't walking on the edge of the curvy, country, chipped, and sealed road. No, she was walking in the middle – not the middle of the lane – smack dab in the middle of the road like she didn't have a care in the world.

I started to panic.

- What happens if a car comes?
- What happens if she's on a blind corner and doesn't have time to move?

As my thoughts started racing out of control, I found myself waving at her to move over. Nothing. No response. Finally, I was standing right in front of her, irritatingly saying, "MOM!" Startled, she jumped and started laughing, letting me know she hadn't seen me. As I started to explain my concerns, I realized she couldn't even see me before. She didn't realize I was there until I was right in front of her, and despite my protestations, she insisted she was fine.

When I think about my mom's lack of peripheral vision, how she can't see anything unless it's right in front of her, and how she is essentially living her life with blinders on, I can't help but think that's exactly how I viewed church, religion, spirituality, and God when I was younger and before I did the hard work of deconstruction. I think back to my time with Embrey, my absolute belief and insistence that I was right, and my inability to see anything other than what I had always been taught.

I was only able to see what the church allowed and trained me to see – what they put right in front of me. I was incapable of seeing beyond those blinders, just like my mom after her traumatic brain injury. It didn't matter what anyone said to me, what logic they used, what Biblical proof they had – I couldn't see past the blinding, limiting theology of the church I had been raised in. If you're in this spot today, then I'd say there's a pretty strong probability you have been in that place, too. Like me, though, something or someone happened that allowed you to catch glimpses of what lay beyond your blinders. Maybe it only took that one glimpse for you to deconstruct, or maybe, like me, it took years of small glimpses and a disastrous catalyst for you to choose deconstruction.

While I'm sure our stories have some similarities and just as many differences, the reality is that we are both here in this place beyond deconstruction, desperately attempting this process of reconstruction. I don't know what it was like for you once the blinders were removed, but for me, it was overwhelming. I limped through the process of deconstructing all the absolutes I had been taught, and after some time, I was able to say what I knew wasn't true, what I had identified as faulty theology, and what I understood as toxic religiosity.

For me, it wasn't so much like I took a wrecking ball to my belief system and was then left to comb through the rubble on my own; instead, it was more like I dismantled it piece by piece. Still, though, I was left with rubble that I was desperate to try to make sense of.

This is the point in so many peoples' deconstruction journeys where many choose to put down roots and stay put. Honestly, I can't say that I blame anyone for that. Deconstruction work is exhausting, and when you've walked through it, the task of rebuilding, reconstructing, renovating, or even just redecorating can feel like too much. There are so many emotions involved, so many hurts and so many obstacles.

I get it. I understand why people get to the end of that journey and think they have no energy for another one, how they arrive at the end of that journey and can't reconcile the hurt they've experienced, the lies they've been told, or the abuse they've endured with the idea that there is a good God in this universe. It's understandable.

If you're here, though, you're feeling that nudge. That's exactly where I was. I walked the road of deconstruction and somehow only lost my faith in certain aspects of humanity without losing my faith in God. I'm guessing that's where you are, too. You've walked the hard road of deconstruction, and somehow, you still have some remnant of faith left.

While it might feel daunting and like something you can't do on your own, I'm here to tell you that it's possible. I want to give you the freedom and permission to breathe again, friend.

To do that, though, it takes an open heart and an open mind. It takes being willing to look at the hard things, the hurts, the open wounds, and the scars, and think deeply about them. It takes looking at your own life and your own choices and identifying why you did those things and made those choices. It's hard work, but it's worthy work.

ON THE DEFENSE

One of the things I struggled with the most at the beginning of my deconstruction journey was seeing the Bible, theology, and traditions through a different lens. I was trained from a young age, birth really, to think a certain way about Biblical and theological principles. Part of that training meant that I was taught not to question the theological tenets of my church. Instead, I was taught to defend our position because our position was the only true position.

The entire approach to theology was based on defense as opposed to offense. I grew up in the rural Midwest, and football was life – second only to God, it seemed, for much of my life. These were the years when high school football in the Midwest involved one short, stout, incredibly strong back who would power forward and smash his way through defenders to secure touchdowns and 100+ yard rushing games weekly. As the opponent facing these teams, the goal for the week was never focused on the offense; it was always focused on the defense – how are we going to stop this running back?

That's the same way my church approached their theology. Instead of focusing primarily on the truth of what they believed, they attacked and schemed against what they considered to be the lies of every other church. So, they taught exactly how to argue against women in leadership. They taught the cherry-picked Scripture passages to use against the churches that didn't believe in full immersion baptism. For every theological difference they had with other churches, they had a defense in place to shut it down.

What that meant for me as an adult was I found it extremely difficult to quiet those voices and dismantle that defensive posture. I was taught to see the world and theology through a very limited lens, and when I took that lens off, I struggled to see anything clearly. I struggled to think for myself beyond the theology I was taught, and, consequently, I struggled to find truth for myself.

For over thirty years, my brain was raised to hear certain words like baptism, women, marriage roles, submission, purity, service, and selflessness, and automatically assume a defensive posture. What I realized as I began to deconstruct these core components of my faith was that I had never considered them outside of the context of my church's teachings.

I didn't know what I didn't know, and I didn't have a new lens I could use to examine these things. I know we all have biases – some conscious and some unconscious. My goal throughout my deconstruction journey, though, was to evaluate the rubble of my faith with as little bias as possible, read the Bible, and analyze my faith for the sole purpose of truth.

That was important to me. It is so easy, and completely understandable, to approach this type of journey with anger, with a ginormous weight on our shoulders, with emotional baggage, with trauma and trauma responses, and with grief. I didn't want to do that, though.

I wanted to read the Bible as literature.

I wanted to see the characters as individuals – as humans.

I wanted to step back and see the Big Picture instead of only focusing on the Scriptures that had been cherry-picked for me over the years to use as a defense.

That meant consciously choosing to strip away my taught theology and open my Bible to read it with clarity and a new purpose.

THE FALL

I was in the middle of my deconstruction journey when I first started to think about the story of Adam and Eve a little differently. There was just something about Eve and her situation that I couldn't shake, something more than everything I had been taught growing up.

Before I ever took the time to read Eve's story on my own without the lens of my childhood, I thought, "Yeah, that sounds about right." However, since I've taken it upon myself to read and study on my own, I've come to see the complexity of this story. There are so many details and aspects of this passage that get overlooked and ignored in churches today. Those details are important, though. Like so many other things, when we ignore those details, the entire narrative changes.

Genesis tells us the story of creation, but then it shifts to the serpent, and we find out that "the serpent was clever, more clever than any wild animal God had made."[1] The exchange between Eve and the Serpent is fascinating. In response to the serpent's question asking if God told them they couldn't eat from any tree in the garden, Eve says:

> "Not at all. We can eat from the trees in the garden. It's only about the tree in the middle of the garden that God said, 'Don't eat from it; don't even touch it or you'll die.'"[2]

I read this, and I think what a harmless response Eve had here, how she must have just genuinely and honestly been answering this question – even though she's talking to a serpent, which, again, I have questions about.

I've heard so many discussions about this scene, so many theologians who split hairs over the exact wording, Eve's actions, and especially over the fact that Eve ate the fruit first. I've heard preachers talk about how Eve was ignorant and didn't know what she was doing, of how the serpent lied to her and twisted God's words to manipulate her.

---

[1] Genesis 3:1 MSG

[2] Genesis 3:2-3 MSG

For years, when I heard this narrative, I heard about the fact that it wasn't until after they ate the forbidden fruit that they realized they were naked and they were ashamed. That point was driven home – their shame was driven deep into my brain. After Adam and Eve ate the fruit of The Tree of Knowledge of Good and Evil, they immediately realized they were naked and were ashamed of their nakedness. They responded how the vast majority of us would respond: they hid, and they attempted to cover themselves.[3] Adam and Eve were familiar with walking in the garden with God. They knew what his presence felt like. They were ashamed for Him to see them naked.

That's the narrative I was taught to believe, and that's the narrative I read before reconstruction. Now, though, I see this narrative a little differently. Look at what happens at the end of this narrative:

"God made leather clothing for Adam and his wife and dressed them."[4]

He made them new clothes – clothes that were more sturdy and better quality than the fig leaves they found for themselves – and He dressed them.

After their choices.

After their failure.

In spite of their shame.

Easing their fears.

When I think about how I felt throughout the deconstruction process, I have to wonder if my feelings weren't similar to what Adam and Eve were feeling when they were hiding from God because they felt ashamed. Even though I knew deconstruction was

---

[3] Genesis 3:7 MSG

[4] Genesis 3:21 MSG

necessary, and I was confident I would finally get to the reconstruction process, there were so many times when I felt ashamed for walking away from the only belief system I knew, like I was hiding from God in case I was wrong, and as if I was holding my breath until I could finally breathe again.

Thankfully, though, when God finds us stripped down and hiding in the bushes, His response is the same for us as it was with Adam and Eve. Despite our choices, despite our failures, despite our shame, and easing our fears – God is there to clothe us and meet our needs – just like he was for Adam and Eve.

I have to think that when God came into the garden and Adam and Eve were hiding, those moments felt like hours as they sat and waited for what they assumed would be death. I wonder how long it took Adam and Eve to start to breathe again, to finally feel the weight begin to rise off their shoulders as their hearts slowed back down.

Maybe that's how you feel too – like you've been holding your breath for days, months, maybe even years – waiting for that moment when the weight finally lifts and you can breathe again. I pray that today is the day that you step out from behind the bush, dust yourself off, and give yourself permission to start breathing again.

THE HUNT FOR TRUTH

As I've analyzed this scene, trying to understand the different dynamics of personalities and relationships, I can never get past the fact that Eve knew God intimately. She spent time walking with Him in the garden; she knew the sound and feel of His presence in her life.

And yet...

Despite her relationship with God, her intimacy with Him, and the hours she spent with her Creator, Eve still longed to know more and desired truth. That was what sealed the deal for Eve when she was met with the words of the serpent – knowledge and truth.

That's precisely where I found myself during deconstruction and throughout my reconstruction as well.

I knew God.

I had walked with God.

I knew the sound and the feel of His presence.

But I was desperate for knowledge and truth.

Even though that quest and journey have sometimes led me to places of fear and shame, God has continually clothed me and covered that shame for me.

And I know He'll do the same thing for you as you begin, or maybe continue, on this journey of reconstruction, feel the weight of your church hurt, spiritual abuse, or faulty theology begin to lift off your shoulders, find a place to call home and begin to breathe again.

REFLECTIONS: BREATHING DEEPLY

Remember:

- Being able to breathe again is a process.

- Finding a place where you feel at home doesn't happen overnight.

- Deconstruction is a process, but reconstruction is a process as well.

- Reconstruction begins with acknowledging the lens, bias, and lack of peripheral vision you were raised with.

- Eve knew God intimately, but she was still desperate for knowledge and truth.

- After God found Adam and Eve naked, He clothed them.

Receive:

Revelation 21:3-5 TPT

And I heard a thunderous voice from the throne, saying: "Look! God's tabernacle is with human beings. And from now on he will tabernacle with them as their God. Now God himself will have his home with them— 'God-with-them' will be their God! He will wipe away every tear from their eyes and eliminate death entirely. No one will mourn or weep any longer. The pain of wounds will no longer exist, for the old order has ceased." And God-Enthroned spoke to me and said, "Consider this! I am making everything to be new and fresh. Write down at once all that I have told you, because each word is trustworthy and dependable."

Reflect:

1. What church hurt, spiritual abuse, faulty theology, etc., is weighing you down today?

2. What needs to happen in your life, church, faith community, etc., for you to feel like you can breathe again or maybe breathe for the first time?

3. What rubble from your deconstruction do you have to sort through to begin this process of reconstruction?

4. What fears do you have related to the process of reconstruction?

5. What obstacles stand in your way of this process of reconstruction?

Prayer:

God, this is hard. This journey of deconstruction was hard, and I know what lies ahead of me on this journey of reconstruction is going to be hard as well. I don't have all the answers right now, and I don't even know if I really know all my questions, but I know that I desperately want to find a home and be able to breathe freely. God, my prayer is that you guide me through this process, you help me to see the truth, your truth, separate from any lens or bias I've had in the past. Help me to be able to sit in your presence free of any weight holding me down or causing me not to be able to breathe freely. Walk with me through this process, directing me to peace and understanding.

II

WHEN CHURCH HURTS:
RECOVERING FROM YOUR
RELIGIOUS TRAUMA

I was sitting at my writing desk in the little corner of our master bedroom when I saw Jason's text. Because he's both my cousin and one of my pastors, his texts can be either simple or heavy. One text may ask me if his boys can fish in our pond, and another may ask if I can spare a few minutes to talk to someone in crisis. This one fell somewhere in the middle – he wanted to know if I would be willing to lead a small group.

I've led small groups for several years, but most of the time, they're "non-church-sanctioned" small groups. Those groups happened when God threw a book in my path and then showed me the women I was supposed to invite. They also allowed me to have the occasional glass of wine and not feel bad when I wore my "I love Jesus, but I cuss a little" sweatshirt.

The church knows I have these small groups – mostly because the pastor's wives end up being some of the women who sit in my living room. But when the need arises, and the Holy Spirit is nudging me, I end up leading an actual "church-sanctioned" small group.

When Jason asked me about leading this group, he gave me a solid out. He said he knew I was busy writing my manuscript and that I shouldn't feel pressured – partly because he knows I have a terrible time saying no to things and partly because he knew I legitimately had a ton on my plate at the moment.

After a few days of prayerful consideration, I felt the Holy Spirit's nudge to open my living room and lead this small group.

Several weeks passed as I prayerfully considered several books, and the announcement was made in the church at the end of each service urging folks to sign up. While I have a rule that I don't choose books for small groups that I haven't read yet, I was smack dab in the middle of Carlos Rodriguez's *Drop the Stones* when I had to make the final decision. The book and the Holy Spirit were both tugging at my heart, so I made a split-second decision to go with it.

After the signups were complete and I had my list of names and phone numbers, I realized I only knew three of the 14 people who had signed up. Several of the names on the list I had never even heard of before. As I finished the book and prepared a study guide to send to these virtual strangers, I started to get a little anxious. I am a fan of pushing the envelope, but Carlos Rodriguez takes it to the next level.

As I was reading through his chapters about church hurt, gender roles, LBGTQ+ communities, and abortion, I got even more anxious. If I could have looked into the Holy Spirit's eyes, I would have shouted, "What did you do?"! To make matters worse, the morning before our first small group, our third pastor and his wife informed me they would be joining us, too. To be clear here, we have four pastors in our church. Each pastor has a spouse, and seven out of the eight had signed up for my small group.

The first night of the group arrived, and our living room filled with both new and familiar faces. I facilitate small groups in a sort of round-robin system, allowing everyone a chance to speak about each topic and question. I had no idea what to expect from this group, but as soon as we started the discussion, my mind was completely blown.

Carlos Rodriguez discusses churches throughout several early chapters of *Drop the Stones*, referencing many examples of church hurt. He opens his chapter entitled "Loving the Mess" with a quote from Stephen Colbert, who states, "The church is a flawed and human institution for whom I always have hope."[5] Then Rodriguez speaks of his own thoughts on the church and church hurt. He says:

> No matter how much the church needs to be challenged, my challenge is to keep believing in the church. Not because she's perfect, but because she belongs to Him (and I'm part of her). After my year of death, grave, and resurrection, I began to be aware of many things I had not been aware of before. My eyes were open to both the beauty and the hypocrisy of modern church life. My heart was like a sponge that could absorb the healing that the family of God provided me as much as the madness it inflicted on others. I was shocked at how bipolar my emotions were every Sunday morning, yet after a season of pain and transformation, I began to love the body of Christ again.[6]

As I listened to these folks talk and share their experiences on churches, one thing became abundantly clear: every single person sitting in that circle had experienced church hurt or religious trauma in one form or another, and every one of them related to the

---

[5] Quoted in Carlos Rodriguez "Drop the Stones." Rodriguez, Carlos. "9: Loving the Mess." *Drop the Stones*, Whitaker House, Kensington , PA, 2017.

[6] Rodriguez, Carlos. "9: Loving the Mess." *Drop the Stones*, Whitaker House, Kensington , PA, 2017.

emotions Carlos speaks about related to their individual bipolar feelings on Sunday mornings.

Some of us had been hurt by damaging church theology, others had been hurt by people in the church who were guided by damaging theology. Still others were injured by narcissistic leaders and abusers in the church, and some of us had suffered from all three. I was speechless at how God had brought together this seemingly random group of people who needed healing in many of the same areas.

TEARING OUT THE WEEDS

I first began to understand healing when I was working through my divorce. I spent a year in weekly therapy sessions. My therapist was the polar opposite of me in every way, shape, and form. Somehow, this made him the perfect therapist for me. I needed someone with a different perspective to be able to listen to me, empathize with me, assure me I wasn't crazy, and help me get to the roots of my dysfunction. Therapy was life-changing for me, and I would be lying to you if I told you I didn't recommend therapy to every single person who crosses my path regardless of what's going on in their life.

One week, I was struggling with a particularly messy season of my divorce. I questioned my sanity, wondering if my responses and reactions were causing even more problems and if there was something I needed to be doing differently. I remember explaining the situation in detail to my therapist, ready to pull my hair out. He listened quietly and paused a minute after I finished before explaining that some people refuse to accept reality. He said that some people are so confident in the reality they created that even if you had video footage of an event, they would still argue it wasn't true; they believe what they believe regardless of the facts.

That was an "aha" moment for me as I went through my divorce–the moment when I was able to see the root of the dysfunction I was dealing with. It was the catalyst for me to analyze and determine the root of the dysfunction that had plagued my marriage.

It was hard work.

It was work that gave me the foundation I needed to be able to apply those same principles to the dysfunction I experienced in my church. For the first time in my life, I was able to take a step back from the church itself, see reality, and understand that even though I was staring that reality straight in the face, other people could look at my reality and argue that it wasn't true because "they believe what they believe regardless of the facts."

That was the root of the dysfunction in my church.

Through therapy, I've learned that issues, problems, and challenges are like weeds in a flower bed. As my grandma neared her 90th year, she finally was at the point where she physically couldn't get down on the ground to weed her flower beds. To be completely honest with you, I hate weeding flower beds. It's not that I hate getting dirty; I'm just terrible at it. It makes my back hurt, and it feels like the seventh circle of hell to me. But when your 90-year-old grandma wants her flower beds cleaned out so she can have something pretty to look at, you weed her flower beds – all four of them.

I know full well that the key to weeding flower beds and keeping the weeds from coming back is making sure you aren't just ripping out what's above the ground. The key is making sure you pull out the roots, too. The problem I had with my grandma's flower beds was that there were so many roots that I had trouble telling the difference between the flowers and the weeds. Consequently, when I started to pull out the weeds and tried to get their roots, flowers would inevitably come, too.

It was a time-consuming and exhausting process.

You might be feeling the same way about your faith. This is the part of the journey where you pull the weeds from your theology and attempt to get to the root of your church hurt, religious trauma, and desire for deconstruction and, now, reconstruction.

It is a tedious and exhausting process.

Just like me in my grandma's flower beds, at times, you might find yourself pulling out some flowers with the weeds. Other times, you might feel like you'll never be able to get all the roots. Eventually, with enough time, energy, and patience, you can do it. You can rid your garden of the weeds.

Cleaning up my Garden

Throughout my deconstruction journey, I found myself questioning the various tenets of my church's theology that shaped my adolescent and early adult years. During that part of my journey, my gut reaction was to "burn it all to the ground." I was angry that I'd spent so many years believing all of these ideas that were presented to me as gospel, only to find out years later they weren't gospel at all.

It wasn't until my reconstruction journey that I took the time to assess the damage each of these tenets caused in my life and to pull them out of my life once and for all – by their roots. If you've gone through therapy for any other trauma in your life, then you know the importance of identifying the trauma and getting to the root of it. It's not enough just to identify the traumatic event and move on. That can cause any number of residual effects. Church hurt and religious trauma are no different. For healing to happen, we have to acknowledge the trauma, accept it as trauma, and work through the results of the trauma.

While I recognize that each journey is different and the tenets that affected me might not be the same ones that affected you, I pray that as you read through my discussion, you can start to think about the ones you identify with, the ones you don't, and the ones that I didn't mention but are still weeds in your garden.

For me, these were the main tenets I had to pull out by the roots:

The Five-Finger Plan of Salvation[7]

I wish I could remember how old I was when I learned the Five-Finger Plan of Salvation, but I know I was young because I was in Dorothy Underwood's Sunday School class, and she only taught kids who were early elementary-aged. Suffice it to say that I learned this little illustration at a very young age.

It went like this, and yes, I had to Google it because I've blocked it out of my memory now:

1. Believe with your mind that Jesus is Lord and He is the only one that can save you.
2. Confess with your mouth that you are a sinner who needs Jesus.
3. Repent of your sins in your heart.
4. Be immersed in Christian baptism for the forgiveness of your sins and the gift of the Holy Spirit.
5. Live a Christian life.

Along with these steps to salvation, the church had specific scriptures they would attach to each to prove their validity.

I've come to accept that most things in the church began with good intentions. This probably started as a simple tool that eventually turned into a doctrine. Unfortunately, this tool taught me and the other kids who were learning it that our salvation was based on a checklist. There was no discussion about any type of relationship with God and no love involved. Instead, the whole of our Christian lives was summed up in five steps that we could check off as we completed them.

7 Garrett, Leroy. *The Stone-Campbell Movement: The Story of the American Restoration Movement.* College Press Publishing, 1981

Baptism

One of my first memories related to baptism was sitting at the table as my older brother talked to the preacher of our small country church about the fact that he wanted to be baptized. He was in fifth grade, and I was in second. I sat and listened to them talk, and I spoke up and said I wanted to be baptized, too. My parents, lovingly, told me I was too young.

That didn't make any sense to me at the time because we were taught from birth that full immersion was necessary for the forgiveness of our sins and the gift of the Holy Spirit. Also, though, we were taught that we could not go to heaven if we were not baptized in this manner. Sprinkling didn't count. Infant baptism wasn't acceptable. Even baptism in a church of another denomination was questionable.

Performance

I grew up believing that favor with God and His love for me had to be earned. It had more to do with our performance than our individual and personal relationships with God. It was about what we brought to the table instead of the fact that God welcomed us to the table. Grace might as well have been a potty word in the church because the focus was on what we could do for God instead of what God was doing for us and in us.

Selflessness

In the church, there was such a prominent focus on Christ's selflessness in His sacrifice for us. Because our goal was to be like Christ, we were encouraged to practice selflessness in all areas of our lives—our relationships, our service, our work, and the church. Any focus on ourselves instead of others was considered to be counter to the example of Christ and, consequently, selfish.

Purity Culture

The 80s and 90s were the heyday of purity culture. It was such a strange time when "abstinence-only" education wasn't just a curriculum for the church but also a curriculum in schools. The message of purity culture and abstinence-only education curriculum were so entwined – the church taught that God wouldn't bless a marriage of anyone who had sex before they were married, while the schools were teaching that sex before marriage would assuredly cause heartache and STDS. In fact, one full day of health class was dedicated to watching slides of pictures of STD infections in people – actual pictures, not cartoons or illustrations. Both the school and the church taught that to have sex before marriage was to give all of yourself away and have nothing left to give a future spouse.

There are entire books devoted to purity culture and the damage caused by purity culture. In a nutshell, the purity culture I grew up in emphasized abstinence before marriage, the responsibility of females to dress and act in a way that didn't cause males to lust, the belief that if you had sex before marriage God would never bless your marriage, the passing out of pledge cards where you could commit to abstinence before marriage, and the belief in secondary virginity (the idea that if you had sex before marriage, you could pray for God to restore your virginity, thus giving you a "secondary virginity").

Let Go and Let God

My upbringing didn't focus on or even preach predestination, but there was an underlying understanding that we had no control over our own lives. God had complete control over each of our lives. Since God was in control and the Bible teaches that we shouldn't worry, to be a good Christian, we had to let go of our worry, anxiety, and desire for control and trust God to bring His will to fruition in our lives–whatever that may be. Our primary responsibility was to release any desire for individual control, agency, and change, and instead, just let God be God.

Pray About It

The most common phrase I heard uttered from the mouths of adults and leaders growing up was "Pray about it." Whenever a person faced a stressful situation, they were encouraged to "Pray about it." Other people would also encourage them by explaining how they would "pray about it" for them. There was no focus on legitimately helping others or seeking help for yourself other than the all-encompassing idea of sitting and "praying about it."

Authority Umbrella

There was an often-spoken and constantly implied belief that God was the authority over man, man was the authority over the church and women, and women could only be the authority over children. It was the role of men to submit to God, women to submit to men, and children to submit to women. As a result, women had no leadership roles in the church, were forbidden from being pastors, and could only teach boys who were not yet considered to be adults.

Heaven and Hell

Becoming a Christian wasn't about loving God and striving to be like Jesus as much as it was about ensuring we would go to heaven after we die instead of burning for an eternity in Hell. The inspiration and motivation for everything we did in the church and our lives was to make sure we made it to heaven and didn't go to hell.

Everyone Else is Wrong

Our church had a predominant underlying belief that everyone who was not part of the "brotherhood" was wrong. Only the members of the churches that belonged to this specific brotherhood of believers would be in heaven.

When I weed my flower beds, I can't always tell if a plant is a flower that's supposed to be there or a weed that needs to be pulled. As my reconstruction journey continues, I sometimes stumble on other ideas and tenets I'm not entirely sure about. I have to decide whether they're weeds that need to be pulled out by the roots or flowers that haven't quite grown into their beauty yet. As you work through this journey, some of the tenets you need to pull out by the roots will be obvious to you, but be patient with yourself and give yourself grace as you patiently analyze the others that aren't so clear to you at first.

THE QUEST FOR TRUTH

Early one morning, I heard my phone vibrate. Bleary-eyed, I picked up the phone to a panicked message from my friend, Missy.

The first text read, "I'm a failure as a mother." Thinking something life-altering had happened, I responded with the most encouraging thing I could come up with, considering it was early and my brain wasn't firing on all cylinders yet: "???"

Missy explained that her daughter, Grace, had lost a tooth. Before the tooth fairy could make her way into Grace's room with the obligatory cash, Missy fell asleep on the couch. Half asleep and forgetting she was supposed to transform into the tooth fairy, Missy fell into bed. It was only in the morning, when Grace came into her room crying, that Missy realized she had forgotten to trade out the tooth for the money.

Being the very creative perfectionist that she is, Missy set out to right this egregious wrong. For the next year, whenever Grace would lose a tooth, the tooth fairy would come to Grace's room while she was sleeping and leave long notes, fairy dust, and exceptionally elaborate scenes for Grace to find in the morning.

The funny part about this entire story is that Grace was old enough to know the tooth fairy didn't exist. She didn't believe in Santa any longer, but for some reason, she was holding on to hope that the tooth fairy was real. It made me laugh because my daughter Kate was the same way. For years after she quit believing in Santa, she insisted on the existence of the tooth fairy.

I thought it was absurd when Kate went through it because she was a logical kid. Even when I gave her all the logical reasons why the tooth fairy could not be real, she continued to argue with me and hold on to that belief. It finally got to be so bad that I would literally have the money in my hand that I was going to put under her pillow, and she still wanted to argue with me and tell me I was just teasing her.

For a hot minute, I started to think this was the hill she was going to die on because she absolutely refused to hear what I was saying, see logic, or believe the facts that were right in front of her. Finally, though, she gave in. She conceded. She admitted that she knew the tooth fairy wasn't real and was just holding on to that one piece of her childhood for as long as she could.

Often, we can be guilty of doing the same thing that Grace and Kate were doing with the tooth fairy when it comes to the tenets of our faith. It can happen for a variety of reasons. The foundation of this issue for me rested in the fact that I had been raised on cherry-picked Scripture passages, so I struggled greatly with both context and reading the rest of those books and stories the cherry-picked Scriptures came from. I was clenching my fists so tightly around some of those Scripture passages and tenets that it took God prying my fingers open before I could release them.

One of the things that helped me release my grip on some of these tenets was reading. I engaged with works by Sarah Bessey, Brian McLaren, and Rachel Held Evans. One of the books that helped me the most was Rachel Held Evans's book *Inspired*. In it, Evans explains:

> The truth is, you can bend Scripture to say just about anything you want it to say. You can bend it until it breaks. For those who count the Bible as sacred, interpretation is not a matter of whether to pick and choose, but how to pick

and choose. We're all selective. We all wrestle with how to interpret and apply the Bible to our lives. We all go to the text looking for something, and we all have a tendency to find it. So the question we have to ask ourselves is this: are we reading with the prejudice of love, with Christ as our model, or are we reading with the prejudices of judgment and power, self-interest and greed? Are we seeking to enslave or liberate, burden or set free?[8]

That one statement illuminated how I had been taught to read Scripture and challenged me to read it differently. I had been taught to read Scripture with the prejudice of judgment, power, self-interest, and greed, not love, and definitely not with Christ as my model.

I committed to reading Scripture differently, focusing on what Jesus did and said, and doing my best to understand the context and culture of the stories I was reading instead of trying to make application to today's world.

It was life-changing.

The irony is that I have a BA and MA in literature (essentially undergraduate and graduate degrees in literary analysis), but I refused to apply those same skills to Scripture until after this experience with Rachel Held Evans.

I started to go through each of these tenets and compare them to what I know about Jesus, who He was, and what He taught. I tried to determine the origin of the rule and how it had morphed and been manipulated over time. Finally, I researched whether any aspect of the tenet held truth or if I was just holding on to it like Kate and Grace held on to the tooth fairy.

This is my challenge to you, friend: arm yourself with information. Read the work of these amazing authors who can help

---

[8] Rachel Held Evans, *Inspired: Slaying Giants, Walking on Water, and Loving the Bible Again*

you understand how to read Scripture critically and how to understand its culture and context. Then, go about the hard work of sorting through the rubble left over from your deconstruction to determine what is true and what is not. It's only then that you can have both peace and an understanding of the impact those tenets have had on your life.

Once I understood the faults, untruths, manipulations, and misgivings of each of these tenets, I went about the difficult work of identifying the damage each had done in my life.

DAMAGE DONE

After identifying the beliefs I had to pull out by the roots, I faced the painstaking job of working through the havoc those tenets had wreaked throughout my life. It was another daunting process. While I have been able to identify many of the larger catastrophes, I still find myself realizing there are more damaged areas I haven't dealt with yet.

It helps me tremendously to write about these things, to sit with a physical journal and pour my thoughts out. Sometimes, I feel like I'm yelling at God, and other times, I feel more like I'm writing to myself or a younger version of myself. The process of writing down the damage allows me to take the power back for myself, begin to release it, and heal from it.

I love pretty journals, and I have a shelf full of them devoted to different things in my life, but I have one dedicated just to the healing I've done and am still doing from my church upbringing. This works wonders for me, and maybe it will help you, too. But if writing isn't your thing, maybe there's someone in your circle you can trust with these things who will hold space for you while you talk through them. If you don't feel safe in that environment just yet, there are amazing therapists out there who can walk through this with you.

We all have had different experiences in the church. The tenets that governed my early church experiences might have some
similarities to yours, but they also might differ greatly. I would
encourage you to go back to your journey of deconstruction and
reflect on the beliefs you have deconstructed and deemed to be
false, destructive, misconstrued, and/or manipulated. Dissect
those. Break them down. Weigh them against what you know to
be true from Scripture, historical texts, experts in that field, etc.
Then, you can determine if any aspect of that tenet contains truth
and reconstruct from there, or you can eliminate it from your faith
journey completely.

Much like our tenets may differ, the damage caused by them
might differ as well. I hope, though, that as you read through the
areas I've identified in my own life, it helps you think through the
damage you see from your own deconstructed beliefs.

Constantly Monitoring My Behavior
I still struggle with the guilt that comes from my inner questioning. I wonder if I'm doing enough or if I'm ever going to be good
enough. Even though I know these questions are remnants of my
past religious life, they still sneak up on me at the strangest times.
They tend to rear their ugly heads whenever there is a need that
I know I can fill. Instead of sitting with the need and listening to
God's nudges, my gut reaction is always to be the first to volunteer. I know that's because this was the expectation I lived in for
so many years of my life, but it is an incredibly difficult impulse
for me to shut off. Worse, when I do say no because I know I'm
not supposed to do whatever is needed, I struggle with feeling like
I'm a bad person or I'm never going to be good enough for God to
love me!

When I don't volunteer to fill the need or if anything even
remotely negative happens in my world or to my loved ones, I still
find myself questioning if God is punishing me for saying no. I still

struggle to get my heart and mind to believe the truth that God loves me unconditionally and doesn't punish me for not performing the way the church taught me I had to perform or practicing the selflessness I was raised to believe was essential to being like Christ.

So much of this process is reigning in my thoughts when they begin to take off out of control. Therapy helped me learn how to grab those thoughts and filter them through what I know is true. Now that I know God doesn't punish me for saying no and that He loves me unconditionally, I can compare those wayward thoughts with what I know is true and shut them down more quickly than in the past. It takes work, though, and diligence to keep my thoughts under control and not let those old theologies of my past overcome the truth.

I love this encouragement from Colossians 3:

You are always and dearly loved by God! So robe yourself with virtues of God, since you have been divinely chosen to be holy. Be merciful as you endeavor to understand others, and be compassionate, showing kindness toward all. Be gentle and humble, unoffendable in your patience with others. Tolerate the weaknesses of those in the family of faith, forgiving one another in the same way you have been graciously forgiven by Jesus Christ. If you find fault with someone, release this same gift of forgiveness to them. For love is supreme and must flow through each of these virtues. Love becomes the mark of true maturity.

Let your heart be always guided by the peace of the Anointed One, who called you to peace as part of his one body. And always be thankful.[9]

---

[9] Colossians 3:12-15 TPT

There are no conditions on God's love for me. He always loves me, and His virtues are mercy, compassion, kindness, gentleness, humility, and patience. He tolerates my weakness and forgives me graciously because love is supreme and flows through him–regardless of how I perform, how I act, or how weak I am.

Fear of Hell

Because of the focus on earning our way to heaven and avoiding the fires of hell, I grew up with an exceptionally unhealthy fear of hell. When I was seven, there was a terrible thunderstorm that woke me up in the middle of the night and I was convinced it was the trumpets and Jesus was coming back. I was terrified that I'd forgotten to ask for forgiveness for just one of my sins and that that would keep me from going to heaven, sending me straight to hell.

The fear didn't end as I got older though. For years, before I went to sleep at night, I would pray a blanket prayer asking God to forgive me of all of my sins – just to cover any I might have forgotten in my other prayers throughout the day.

It wasn't just a fear for my own soul that scared me, though; it was a fear of hell for the souls of my loved ones. What if *they* had forgotten to ask forgiveness for any of *their* sins? What if they died when they were speeding on the highway and went to hell?

This thinking creeps back in sometimes. It rears its ugly head the most when people pass away, and I don't know anything about their relationship with God. I question whether they're in heaven or hell and revert to all of those teachings that scarred me throughout my childhood.

Then, I remember life is not a test to see if we can make it to heaven and get a reward. The kingdom of heaven Jesus spoke about is here and now. Some great scholars write about this, but one of my favorite authors who writes on this topic of the kingdom of heaven vs heaven and hell is Rob Bell.

In *Love Wins,* Bell writes:

To say it again, eternal life is less about a kind of time that starts when we die, and more about a quality and vitality of life now in connection to God.

Eternal life doesn't start when we die; it starts now. It's not about a life that begins at death; it's about experiencing the kind of life now that can endure and survive even death."[10]

I've come to understand God didn't create us to chase heaven; He created us to bring the kingdom of heaven to earth.

Struggling to Believe Love Is Not Conditional

I spent so many years believing that God would only love me and bless my life if I was doing what I was supposed to be doing. The minute I messed up or sinned, I feared God would snatch His love and favor from my life, and I would end up being just like the Israelites who died before they could ever enter The Promised Land. Consequently, I was on this constant roller coaster of trying to be who I thought God wanted me to be and do what I thought God wanted me to do to attempt to earn His love.

It didn't just end with God, though. Those beliefs transferred to people; if we were created in God's image, then I believed that people must look at me in that same way. That meant that people would only love me if I was doing what I was supposed to be doing and acting the way I was supposed to be acting. I desperately feared disappointing anyone. I thought they would take their love away from me if I didn't do what they asked or expected of me. This led to being a people-pleaser in every aspect of my life, constantly overcommitting and always being afraid of the fallout that would inevitably come if I said no.

[10] Rob Bell, *Love Wins: A Book About Heaven, Hell, and the Fate of Every Person Who Ever Lived*

Now, I find myself encouraged by this truth from Romans 8:

> So now I live with the confidence that there is nothing in the universe with the power to separate us from God's love. I'm convinced that his love will triumph over death, life's troubles, fallen angels, or dark rulers in the heavens. There is nothing in our present or future circumstances that can weaken his love. There is no power above us or beneath us—no power that could ever be found in the universe that can distance us from God's passionate love, which is lavished upon us through our Lord Jesus, the Anointed One![II]

I can't make God love me more, and I can't make Him love me any less. His love is constant and consistent– regardless of what I do, who I am, or what troubles life throws at me.

Lack of My Own Identity

I spent my adolescence being taught that my entire identity was Christ alone. It was considered selfish to have my own wants and desires beyond Christ. Because Scripture says that we are to pour ourselves out and fill ourselves up with Christ, I was taught that any remnant of my own identity apart from Christ was sinful and a symbol of living for the self instead of the Spirit.

This lack of identity and complete inability to identify my own wants and needs was detrimental in many, if not all, of my relationships. While therapy helped tremendously, I still often struggle to even identify what I want and need, let alone communicate it to others.

I'm still a work in progress.

When I'm having trouble advocating for myself or accepting my own needs, it's helpful for me to remember God made each

---

[II] Romans 8:38-39 TPT

of us mysteriously complex. In Psalm 139, David praises God for making him mysteriously complex.[12] I am no different. I have my own identity and complexities just like David did. That complexity means my needs, my personality, and my identity are unique to me, and no one else has them.

Denial of Self-Care

There was such a strong emphasis in my church on the idea that because Christ was selfless, we were supposed to be selfless. Consequently, any individual needs we expressed made us selfish, which was the opposite of Christ. These needs were dismissed and treated as unimportant because Christ should be all we need in our lives. We were never to even speak of self-care, mental health treatment, or individual agency. Those were all things that made us selfish and showed weak faith because Jesus should be all we need.

You can imagine how damaging it could be to live life with no acknowledgment of the need to take care of and love yourself, acknowledge mental health, or have agency over your life. For me, it looked like constantly running myself ragged to overachieve and pouring myself into everyone and everything else. It looked like never having the ability to say "no" when I was asked to do something.

Then I learned that Jesus commonly left the crowds and went off by Himself to rest, pray, and take care of Himself.[13] I have to give myself permission to rest just like Jesus gave Himself permission. Christ prioritized His rest, and I should do the same.

Inability to Set Boundaries

I spent nearly 40 years of my life as the dictionary definition of codependent. I couldn't set a boundary with anyone because boundaries seemed selfish to me. I was taught that it was my

---

[12] Psalm 139:14 TPT

[13] Matthew 8:23-26, Mark 4:35-41, Mark 1:35, Matthew 14:13, Mark 6:31-32, Matthew 15:29

God-given role in life to be selfless and take care of everyone else, regardless of who they were and what they were doing. Consequently, not only could I not set a boundary, I couldn't even wrap my head around what boundaries looked like. They seemed like the antithesis of Christlike living to me and that was the opposite of who I wanted and needed to be in my life.

I've spent countless hours studying who Christ was, what He did, and what He taught when He was on earth. I've learned that Christ had His boundaries on display for us to emulate throughout his ministry. I love how the Pharisees constantly questioned Him and His disciples, but instead of engaging with anger, Jesus simply answered with His own questions or simple statements. He didn't offer opportunity for argument. Another boundary He set was in how he separated Himself from crowds when He needed to be alone, rest, or pray—even when it was His inner circle He was distancing Himself from. This inner circle was yet another boundary He set. He only invited certain people into His inner circle and still separated Himself from them when He needed to recharge.

The more I learn about Jesus, the more I understand that He was the opposite of codependent in His relationships. While He preached love, He also practiced self-care and self-love. More than anything else, this knowledge has helped me set healthy boundaries in my life.

One of the best books I've read on boundaries is Lysa TerKeurst's *Good Boundaries and Goodbyes*. In it, she discusses the necessity of implementing boundaries, how boundaries have always been in God's plan for us, and how to say goodbye to relationships in a healthy way. She offers an in-depth discussion of how boundaries are from God. One of my favorite things she taught me is that "Boundaries aren't just a good idea, they are a God idea."[14]

---

[14] Lysa TerKeurst, *Good Boundaries and Goodbyes: Loving Others Without Losing the Best of Who You Are*

Misunderstanding Sexuality

Purity culture was possibly one of the most detrimental and debilitating aspects of my church upbringing. As an adolescent, I was never allowed to understand my sexuality because I was taught as a woman that my sexuality was dangerous and should be hidden. In terms of sex itself, I was raised to believe that men thought about sex all the time – so much so that we were given statistics on how many times males think about sex per minute! Because of a man's inability to control his thoughts, we as women were charged with the task of never doing anything to "make them lust."

We were also taught that women were "wired completely differently" than men. Women didn't have the same sex drive as men and should always be the ones to stay in control of any situation that might tempt a man to behave badly.

The amount of pressure I felt as a woman to control how I dressed and how I acted to never "be a stumbling block" to my "Christian brothers" is absurd. This pressure, coupled with the guilt of never being able to live up to these unrealistic and ridiculous standards of thought and behavior, unraveled me. They especially unraveled me after I got married, and all those promises of a perfect life and amazing sex were never fulfilled.

These misconceptions were so extreme that only professional therapy helped me dismantle the lies and approach sexuality in a healthy, fulfilling, honest, and authentic manner. Since then, I've found several fantastic resources to help dismantle the damage purity culture has inflicted. Cara and Rachel at healthywholeway.com are both former pastors who walked away from their previous beliefs and ways of life, dedicating their lives to helping others heal. They have fantastic resources and a great community for support.[15]

---

[15] https://www.happywholeway.com/

Mistrust of Self

I spent years in churches that taught me that I was broken, only God could fix me, and that I was a product of depravity who needed to be saved from myself and my terrible thoughts and decisions. This mindset instilled a constant mistrust of my ability to think critically, solve my problems, and trust my gut. In fact, the only time I was taught I was able to trust my gut was when it was the Holy Spirit speaking to me through my gut. But no one taught me how to discern when it was the Holy Spirit speaking to me through my gut! Consequently, I constantly questioned what was behind my gut reaction: Spirit or self.

"The Happy Whole Way" offers a discussion of how this religious programming affects us and the steps we can take to retrain our brains. They explain:

> Religious programming is the aftereffect of the teachings and indoctrinations of religion that defined for you how to:
>
> View the world (us vs. them)
>
> Behave among your community and the outside world around you (the rules of behavior)
>
> Relate to yourself (you are sinful, in need of saving)
>
> It leaves deeply lasting effects on your life, your thought patterns, and your emotional wellbeing; and how you operate in the world now has been greatly influenced by your religious programming.
>
> And the kicker about religious programming is that it doesn't just leave you once you've left the Church. This stuff will unconsciously keep playing behind the scenes, unknowingly guiding you.[16]

---

[16] https://www.happywholeway.com/blog/what-exactly-is-religious-programming

To escape this programming, I had to understand why I didn't trust myself, then I had to dismantle that programming, and finally remember, again, that God created me with my own unique, mysterious, and complex identity. Once I was able to rest in that truth, I was able to get past my mistrust of myself. It didn't happen overnight, though.

Skewed Perception of Marital Roles

I'd have to say it's a toss-up between purity culture and how I was taught to view marital roles for "what teaching damaged me the most." I spent the first several decades of my life being taught that women were never to be in positions of authority above men. This teaching was so literal that women weren't even allowed to teach Sunday School classes that had males present over the age of 18.

That same perception of the roles of men and women transferred into marriage. I was taught that it was my job to support my husband regardless of his actions. It was considered disrespectful for a woman to question anything a man did, and it would have been a mortal sin for a woman to criticize her husband or talk about his faults with anyone else. It was a pretty standard practice that the word "divorce" should never be spoken. There was some skewed ideology that suggested if you suffered quietly in marriage and never said the word divorce out loud, divorce would never happen.

According to purity culture, once you were married, everything would magically just click into place sexually, and couples would have amazing sex lives because God would bless them exponentially for following His plan for marriage. Within that same teaching, though, was the ideology that men wanted sex all the time, and it was the role of the wife to provide for her husband sexually. I remember an older woman in my church growing up who claimed she had never told her husband "no" when he wanted sex. There was a blatant disregard for women and their needs – any needs. The sole focus of marriage and sexuality was on men and how the women could meet the men's needs.

This is especially troublesome as a survivor of purity culture because I had been raised for twenty years to believe that women weren't supposed to be sexual, always cover themselves, and never tempt a man. Somehow, I was supposed to forget all of those teachings when I became a wife and miraculously become the perfect sexual partner.

The amount of logical fallacies present in this teaching is astronomical, creating completely unrealistic expectations for marriage, sex, and sexuality. I've spent years working through this, and I still feel like I've only scratched the surface of my healing. I've dismantled and approached this the same way as I have each tenet – weighed these thoughts and beliefs against the model of who Jesus was and how He taught love. I've also utilized professional therapy to rewire how my brain thinks about marriage and relationships.

HEALING IS A JOURNEY

One thing I've realized over these years of deconstruction and reconstruction is that as soon as I think I've healed in one area, another wound opens up. I can be sitting in church, reading a book, or even just in the middle of a conversation with a friend, and I'll feel like I've been hit by a ton of bricks.

It was in those minutes that I remember this is a journey and that I still have work to do. In these moments, I don't consider myself broken or weak; instead, I just kind of think of myself as a sojourner who isn't quite done with this journey yet.

I'm grateful for these tools that I learned in therapy, just as I'm thankful for the critical thinking skills I've learned along the way and the constant guidance of the Holy Spirit, who knows me intimately.

This is hard work – the dismantling of the tenets of your faith and the acknowledgment that the people we loved, the churches we served in, and the leaders we respected both allowed and even perpetuated this damage we are now working through.

It's also hard work to look at our lives through a lens of healing and painstakingly identify the damage that has resulted from church hurt, spiritual abuse, and religious trauma.

I'm so grateful for the healing work I've done and the ability to understand why I react the way I do in certain situations. While I know this is a difficult part of the journey, I pray you take the time to sit down with God or a therapist, or God and a therapist, and you begin to name the damage and the hurt you endured. When you do that, you can begin to take the power back for yourself and take the power away from your abuser/church/theology, etc.

Today is that day, friend.

Today is the first day of your journey to reclaim your power and release the hold this has had on your life.

If this step of the journey is too heavy for you to carry on your own, there are amazing therapists out there who will walk with you, guide you, and help you. There's no shame in seeking professional help. As Carlos Rodriguez says, "You can love Jesus and still see a therapist."[17]

---

[17] Rodriguez, Carlos. "24: Whatever You Need to Do." *Drop the Stones*, Whitaker House, Kensington , PA, 2017, pp. 124.

REFLECTIONS: WHEN CHURCH HURTS

Remember:

- The majority of the people in the church and who have left the church have dealt with church hurt and/or religious trauma: you are not alone.
- Tearing out the weeds can feel like a never-ending process.
- When you begin to tear out the weeds, some of the flowers might go with them, too.
- You have to tear out the weeds by their roots to get rid of them completely.
- It takes time to identify and sit with the faulty theology and dangerous tenets that harmed you.
- It's not enough just to identify the faulty theology. The process of identifying how that theology damaged you is an important step toward healing.

Receive:

When you're joined to the Anointed One, circumcision, and religious obligations can benefit you nothing. All that matters now is living in the faith that works and expresses itself through love.

Before you were led astray, you were so faithful. Who has deceived you so that you have turned from what is right?

The One who enfolded you into his grace is not behind this false teaching that you've embraced. Don't you know that when you allow even a little lie into your heart, it can permeate your entire belief system?

Deep in my heart, I have confidence that the Lord, who lives in you, will bring you back around to the truth. And I'm convinced that those who trouble you, whoever they think they are, will bear the penalty (Galatians 5:6-10 TPT)!

Reflect:

1. Spend some time writing out all of the faulty theology and damaging tenets of your previous faith. Be specific. Make sure you take the time to discuss each of them completely. Go back and keep adding to them as you remember more information.

2. For each tenet, spend time reflecting on the damage you experienced as a result of it. Go into as much detail as you can so you can rid yourself of those beliefs completely and begin to heal from them.

Prayer:

God, I pray that you would allow me to see all of the ways I was led astray and damaged by my past. I pray that the Holy Spirit will guide me as I undertake this daunting quest for truth. I pray that you will open my heart and my mind to all that is true, all that is holy, and all that is good. As I attempt to dismantle the damage that has been done to me through faulty theology, I pray that you will allow my heart to be opened and to begin healing. I pray that you would help me to continue to advocate for myself and my healing as I continue on this journey. And, as I begin to think about all of the people and places that contributed to my hurt, I pray that you would help me to work through the seemingly impossible task of forgiveness.

III

BURNING DOWN THE HOUSE:
UNDERSTANDING THE "WHY" BEHIND YOUR DECONSTRUCTION

I looked at the materials my mom had spread out all over our kitchen table: chicken wire, newspaper pieces, some sort of disgusting-looking paste, and ugly brown paint. My 7-year-old brain couldn't wrap my head around what my mom could be doing with all this stuff.

"What are you making?" I asked, and before she had a chance to answer my first question: "Can I help?"

Together, we formed the chicken wire into the most realistic volcano shape we could manage. Then, we started dipping the newspaper pieces into the nasty, slimy paste before we slathered them all over the form.

"It's called paper mache," my mom informed me, "and we're going to make the best volcano ever."

My kid brain didn't care why we were making the best volcano ever. I was just excited I got to help.

We finished layering the newspaper so that every piece of chicken wire was covered, and then we waited for it to dry before painting it the ugliest color of brown I'd ever seen. Thinking our craft project was over, I went to wash my hands and find something else to get into before my mom asked me where I was going and told me we hadn't even done the best part yet.

I was confused because the paper mache volcano looked done to me. Confused, I watched as my mom dropped a few drops of red food coloring into some gross-smelling liquid and then dumped it into the middle of the volcano. I was even more confused when she pulled a box out of the cupboard and spooned a white powder into the volcano's opening.

Immediately, our volcano erupted, and red lava went everywhere. My eyes had to be as big as saucers because A) this was the coolest thing I'd ever seen, and B) My mom was not a fan of messes. As I started to ask a thousand little kid questions, my mom explained she was using the paper mache volcano for her science lesson the upcoming week. She tried to explain to me what that explosion was supposed to be teaching her students, but I was still so intrigued by the red lava flowing I didn't focus much on the "why" behind it.

Blowing things up became a regular theme in our house growing up. Throughout my childhood, my dad was a dirt track race car driver. I heard the term "their engine blew" so many times in my early life, it just seemed like another everyday phrase around my house. It wasn't until my teenage years, when I started driving myself, that I began to question what exactly it meant for an "engine to blow." After all, when this happened, the only external sign was black smoke billowing out of the back of the car and maybe out from under the hood.

My dad explained blown head gaskets, warped heads, and cracks in engine blocks. He explained that most of these issues couldn't be seen from the outside, but the damage they could cause could be irreparable if you weren't diligent in noticing the signs and repairing the root of the issue, not just putting a bandaid on the problem.

FAITH EXPLOSIONS AND IMPLOSIONS

For everyone who deconstructs, there is a moment of explosion or implosion. For some of you, this looks like the volcano did when it exploded on my kitchen table. Something happens, whether in church or out of it, that functions like the baking soda being added to the vinegar. It might not even seem like much to anyone else, but for you, it's the final ingredient for the explosion that results in your deconstruction. It's loud, and everyone around you sees it happening.

For others, though, the catalyst for your deconstruction is more of an implosion. It happens internally more than externally. Just like the motors in the race cars my dad drove, the damage begins on the inside, where the naked eye can't see it. There were probably signs, but you kept slapping bandaids over them and hoping they would go away. Slowly, over time, the damage became worse and worse until, finally, it blew up, leaving a trail of smoke in its wake. Likely, no one else saw the implosion coming. It happened quietly, in your heart and mind, and behind closed doors. Once it blew up, though, there was no longer any hiding it.

What both the explosion and implosion have in common is the endpoint every deconstructor arrives at – the baking soda in the volcano or the crack in the engine block that results in each of us throwing up our hands and saying, "I just can't take this any longer!" Maybe you experienced Sunday School teachings that were so off base you couldn't sit there and listen to them anymore. Maybe the consistent sexism in the church pushed you to your breaking point. Or, maybe you experienced abuse by a pastor or a leader of a church.

For others, though, the catalyst might not even be related to a specific incident in a church. It might have far more to do with what has happened outside of the church with "church people." While several things happened in church over the years that contributed to my implosion, the catalyst itself was realizing I had done "everything right" and gained none of the life the church had promised me I would gain.

This might seem like an odd step for this journey, but for me, identifying that catalyst was one of the most important aspects of both my healing and my reconstruction.

For some people, the catalyst occurs, and the implosion happens quietly. Maybe that's how it happened for you – you started to ask questions in your mind, you went to books, influencers, and the internet to research, but you feared what would happen if you voiced your questions and doubts publicly. So, you sit here today holding this book, recovering from that silent and private implosion and desperately trying to rebuild a faith you have quietly dismantled.

Others, though, have more of a "burn the whole house down" reaction when their faith implodes. That was my reaction, and it was the absolute opposite of my entire personality. For me, the catalyst for my deconstruction/reconstruction was my 18th wedding anniversary–a day that passed, with its only acknowledgement being a text at 10 pm from my husband at the time. That was it for me, the straw that broke the camel's back. You might wonder how this was connected to my deconstruction, but my theology and ideology had driven all of my beliefs and actions related to marriage. I had done everything "right" and reaped none of the rewards, and my entire world came crashing down as a result of it.

We all respond differently to our catalyst. For me, my theology wasn't the only thing that imploded. As the walls of my theology crumbled around me, I realized my entire world, and specifically my marriage, had been built from lies. I blew it up even more. Just a side note, I wouldn't suggest this as the best option or even a viable option, but I was not in a good place to make those decisions at the time. My husband and I had opened a coffee shop four months earlier. I was teaching full time, doing most of the back end and management work at the shop, and working at the shop at least 20 hours a week. I taught four different dual enrollment courses through two universities at a local high school and also taught several high school courses. I was exhausted – mentally, physically, emotionally, and spiritually. When my anniversary came and went without recognition, I was done. My husband and I separated, and months later, I was in a relationship with an 18-year-old coffee shop employee who was also one of my students.

Like I said, I imploded my life completely. The fallout of those decisions was disastrous. I ended up leaving my job, confessing my indiscretions to detectives, and going to prison for a few months before enduring divorce, custody battles, and a complete rebuilding of my life, faith, and relationships from the absolute ground up. Let me reiterate here that this is not the best way to go about deconstructing and reconstructing your faith – or anything else, for that matter. I was lost, felt incredibly alone, and was staring at the complete loss of everything I had ever known dead in the eye.

My old theology told me I was broken, entrenched in shame, lost, beyond grace, and facing nothing but the wrath and anger of God. My reality was that I was flawed, ashamed of my choices, falling headfirst into grace, and enveloped in the loving and redemptive arms of God. Friend, I don't suggest following my path to arrive at this point, but one of the major tenets I learned about God during this time was that He is good, and He truly wants to take everything that the enemy sought to use for evil and make it good. I would have never chosen for God to sit my butt down in prison. I am a consummate rule follower and a huge proponent for justice, so the irony that this was my path and how God showed me grace is not lost on me. I say all the time that the one time I chose to break a rule, I ended up in prison, so no thanks – I'll stick to the rules from here on out!

In that time, though, God revealed Himself to me in ways I never knew possible. I was completely separated from the emotional abuse in marriage and given the freedom (ironic again, I know) to study, be still, and listen to the nudges of the Holy Spirit in a way I never knew possible. During those months "behind the fence," I had the opportunity to read the Bible without the lens of my past theology.

During the first church service I attended behind the fence, I took one of the free Bibles. I had so much free time in those early days, and I was desperate for God to fill the time with His still small voice. My life had been so busy for so many years. I hadn't sat down in the stillness and the quiet with nothing but a pen, some blank paper, my Bible, and God in years. Over the next few weeks, I read, took notes, joined Bible Studies, led Bible Studies, and learned what it was to sit still again, or maybe for the first time in my life.

That separation from everything I thought I knew permitted me to see things differently. I had the freedom and the time to reconstruct my faith with a firm foundation so that even if the walls crumbled again, my foundation would be solid. Even though it is my prayer that your situation looks nothing like mine, I believe that God will provide you with the time and the stillness to be able to do this very thing for your faith.

And that starts today, friend.

A GOD OF REDEMPTION

Your story of deconstruction/reconstruction might not be as implosive as mine – or maybe it is. Regardless of the extent of the implosion, the reality is that our journeys through deconstruction and reconstruction can leave us feeling a myriad of emotions. For some of us, they might involve grave mistakes, guilt over walking away from a church/faith community, fear of judgment, hurt from being disfellowshipped, and/or shame over being viewed as a prodigal – and those are only the tip of the iceberg.

I grew up in the church hearing stories of redemption and sermons from the pulpit lauding God for using everyday, imperfect people all while being criticized and instilled with a fear of hell for being imperfect. While the stories of the Bible are full of grace, my church was void of it. When I took the time to read the Bible through this new lens of grace, I began to understand to what extent God has a history of taking terrible, seemingly impossible situations and revising them for good.

Maybe today is the day you need to look at these stories through a lens of grace so that you can begin to look at your own story that way. God isn't afraid to come down and meet you in the messy middle of your deconstruction and reconstruction.

David

David's story is talked about so often that I worry we lose sight of the intricate details. It's almost as if we forget that the shepherd boy who defeated the giant Goliath is the same teenager who was loved and then hated by Saul, the same King with a warrior's heart, the same man who struggled so much with lust that he sought out and took for himself the married Bathsheba, the same King who had Uriah murdered, the same dad whose son tried to usurp him, the same target of enemy armies, the same humble servant who danced in his underwear, but, ultimately, the same man who was after God's own heart.

The complexity of David's life is convoluted and multi-layered. If we were to peel back each layer, each victory, each defeat, each sin, and each emotion, the one thing that is constant at his core is that he was a man after God's own heart – despite everything else he was.[18] Too often, we become so consumed by perfection and performance, even in deconstruction and reconstruction, that we forget what's most important isn't our wins and losses, our trials and conquests, or our victories and defeats. What's most important is our heart.

When God looked at David, regardless of what was happening in his life at the time, He didn't see a screw-up, a murderer, an adulterer, a rapist, or a warrior. No, when God looked at David, regardless of what was going on in his life at the time, I have to believe God saw David's heart. That's the same thing He sees in you today. When He looks at you, I can't see Him labeling you as someone who gave up on the church, as a doubter, as a prodigal, or as a broken soul. No, when He looks at you today, He sees your heart – the heart that is chasing after truth and desperately trying to find the open air where you can breathe again.

God didn't want David's story to end with all of his failures. He wanted to redeem David's life and his story, and if you are someone who has made some seemingly irreparable decisions on your deconstruction/reconstruction journey, God doesn't look at you and see those. He just looks at you and sees a child He loves with a heart that is for Him. One of the things I love about David's story is that David knew God. He was anointed by Samuel as the next king when he was only a teenage shepherd boy. I Samuel 16:13 says:

> Samuel took his flask of oil and anointed him, with his
> brothers standing around watching. The Spirit of God

---

[18] I Samuel 13:14

entered David like a rush of wind, God vitally empowering him for the rest of his life.[19]

The Spirit of God entered David and empowered him for the rest of his life at this moment. Yet, this roller coaster was still his story. For those of us who have cut our teeth on the back of pews and still made terrible choices – like David – God doesn't look at us any differently than He did David. That's the God my heart is chasing after today, and I'm confident the same is true for you as well.

Tamar

If you aren't familiar with the story of Tamar, let me offer the Cliffs Notes version. You can find the entire account in Genesis 38:

- Jacob's (yes, the same Jacob who had the ambitious, deceptive heart and was the father of the Israelites) son Judah and his wife Shua had a son named Er – he married Tamar.
- Er was evil, so God killed him before he and Tamar had any children.
- Tamar had to marry Er's brother Onan – that was tradition.
- Onan wouldn't have children with Tamar, so God killed him.
- Tamar should have married the third son, but Judah sent Tamar back to her father's house as a widow.
- Penniless and childless, Tamar was desperate.
- After Judah's wife died, she disguised herself as a prostitute and slept with Judah – her father-in-law.
- She kept his staff, seal, and cord for proof of the deed and told him it was collateral until he paid her, but she had no intention of giving them back.

---

[19] I Samuel 16:13 MSG

- Three months later, Judah learned Tamar was pregnant and ordered her to be punished. He didn't know she was the woman he had slept with.
- Tamar revealed his belongings.
- Judah acknowledged his sin and Tamar's righteousness.
- Tamar had twin boys as a result of her encounter with Judah – Perez and Zerah.
- King David and Christ were both descendants of Perez.
- Judah and Tamar are listed by name in Jesus's genealogy.

I have a love/hate relationship with the story of Tamar. I love how God works to redeem and restore her story, but I hate what she has to go through for redemption and restoration to happen. Tamar was a victim of her culture and her circumstances. She had no control over the men she was forced to marry, and she had no control over the fact that her father-in-law wouldn't let his youngest son fulfill his cultural duty to marry her.

I hate that she was in such a place of desperation that she had to dress up as a prostitute to seduce her father-in-law to sleep with her to then blackmail him into doing what he should have done much earlier. And I especially hate that Tamar was forced to bear the child conceived in that union.

What I love about this story is Tamar's tenacity and ingenuity. I love how she uses her resources, gets incredibly creative, and takes matters into her own hands. Even more than that, though, I love how God rewards her and sends Christ through her bloodline despite all the "laws" and "rules" she broke.

Where was a lesson about her in Sunday School? I don't remember seeing a flannel graph of this one.

Sometimes, our circumstances don't fit well into the tightly-constructed box that our churches create, just like Tamar's didn't. Sometimes, we don't fit into that box ourselves. Thankfully, God doesn't change, and His love for us doesn't change because we don't fit in that box anymore. God doesn't love you any less because you're deconstructing/reconstructing, just like He didn't love Tamar any less when she dressed up as a prostitute and had sex with her father-in-law. I don't know about you, but that truth was something I didn't learn in church; however, when I began to understand it, my perception of God and love for His redemption and revision of our stories changed immensely.

Paul

I'm going to go out on a limb here and say that Paul was one of the first deconstruction/reconstruction stories of all time. The irony is that many churches use Paul's words in his letters to first-century churches as a means of oppression and to further drive home their faulty theologies. I wonder what kind of letter Paul would write to those churches today.

I said what I said.

Paul's story is another one that I fear we have heard so many times that we forget the weight of it. He was a Jew – a devout Jew. In many ways, I feel a kinship with Paul in the same way I feel a kinship with David because he would have cut his teeth on the back of a pew, too (if they had pews in the synagogue). Paul was living the way his church and culture told him he should be living. He was so devout that he stood by and watched as Stephen was murdered for heresy. He was following the rules, performing the way he was supposed to be performing, and living the life his church had raised him to live.

The extent of Saul's devotion was extreme. You can see it in how he is introduced before his conversion in Acts 9:

> During those days, Saul, full of angry threats and rage, wanted to murder the disciples of the Lord Jesus. So he went to ask the high priest and requested a letter of authorization he could take to the Jewish leaders in

Damascus, requesting their cooperation in finding and arresting any who were followers of the Way. Saul wanted to capture all of the believers he found, both men and women, and drag them as prisoners back to Jerusalem. So he obtained the authorization and left for Damascus.[20]

I've heard the story of Paul's conversion so many times that the awe and wonder of it sometimes go right over my head without so much as a second thought, and I wonder if you don't find yourself in that same place at times. Paul was traveling on the road to Damascus for the sole purpose of finding and killing Christ's disciples...

Just outside the city, a brilliant light flashing from heaven suddenly exploded all around him. Falling to the ground, he heard a booming voice say to him, "Saul, Saul, why are you persecuting me?"[21]

God literally stopped Paul in his tracks and blinded him with the truth. Talk about a catalyst for deconstruction/reconstruction! That was most definitely a major catalyst, and it caused a massive implosion in Paul's life.

I wonder how Paul's Jewish friends looked at him after his deconstruction/reconstruction. I wonder how many of his former church friends turned their backs on him because he changed his beliefs and behavior. I wonder if he struggled to fit in, to find his voice at first, and to be open and honest about what he was going through.

The one thing that stands out to me about Paul's story – that surely would stand out to me about your story as well – is the fact that God loved Paul enough and cared about his ministry and his

---

[20] Acts 9:1-3 TPT

[21] Acts 9:3-4 TPT

beliefs enough to stop him dead in his tracks and change the trajectory of his life. Maybe that's the message you need to hear today. Maybe you need to know that God loves you and cares about you enough to allow you to dismantle the belief system that was holding you back, causing you pain, or even abusing you.

Paul's life certainly wasn't easy after his deconstruction/reconstruction journey, but it was rich and it was reformed. It most assuredly went in a direction he wasn't planning, but what a blessing for him that it did. Friend, God has you in this place for a reason. He has you on this journey for a reason. It might not be easy right now, and it honestly might not ever be easy, but it will be fresh, and it will be new, and it will be a testament to the revising and reforming power of God.

AFTER THE ASHES SETTLE

I'm not sure where you are on your reconstruction journey. I know this, though: it can be almost impossible to breathe and to see more than a few feet in front of you until after the ashes settle. If you're just starting out on this deconstruction/reconstruction journey, I want to encourage you to stay the course, let the ashes fizzle out and settle, and be patient for the day when you feel like you can finally take a full breath again.

The journey is hard, but it does get easier once you can identify what it is or who it was that was your catalyst for that step into this journey. Then, it gets even more difficult for a while as you learn to navigate through the damage your implosion caused or is possibly even still causing. Just like David, Tamar, and Paul, though, God sees you, sees your heart, and sees that you don't fit into a box well. He is pursuing you and providing you with this opportunity to grow and reconstruct your faith with a foundation that won't fail when it's shaken.

REFLECTIONS: BURNING DOWN THE HOUSE

Remember:

- We all have had different experiences in the church and have different triggers and catalysts for our deconstruction/reconstruction.

- Your catalyst for this process might be something small, like the straw that broke the camel's back or a major traumatic event. Even though those catalysts are different, our journeys are all equally important.

- All of our deconstruction implosions look different, and dealing with the fallout of those implosions is important for the tedious act of reconstruction.

- God has a history of using flawed, devout, out-of-the-box people for good even when they faced situations Satan wanted to use for evil.

- God doesn't love you any less because you are in the process of deconstructing/reconstructing.

Receive:

"Then God raised up deliverers for the people until the time of the prophet Samuel. The people craved for a king, so God gave them one from the tribe of Benjamin: Saul, the son of Kish, who ruled for forty years. After removing him, God raised David up to be king, for God said of him, 'I have found in David, son of Jesse, a man who always pursues my heart and will accomplish all that I have destined him to do.'" (Acts 13:21-22 TPT)

Reflect:

1. What were the moments when you started to question what you believed?
2. What are the specific teachings/traditions you began to question?
3. What specific moments from your church life do you look back on now and see differently than you did at the time?
4. Which of these moments specifically was your catalyst for deconstruction?
5. What happened as a result of your deconstruction? What was the implosion like?
6. What has the fallout been from your implosion?

Prayer:

God, I pray that you would help me to be able to clearly see and identify the moments, teachings, and people who were the catalyst(s) for my deconstruction/reconstruction journey. I pray that you would walk with me through this process and help me to consistently feel your love and the nudges of the Holy Spirit. I pray you would help me to know the truth and be able to use that truth as the foundation for my faith that cannot be shaken – even when the walls are coming down. I pray that you would forgive me for the things I did during the implosion of my faith and that you would continue to revise and reform my story. God, I know that you love me the same today as you did yesterday and that your love never changes. I pray that you would remind me of that when I'm struggling with my faith or with dismantling aspects of my faith I thought true in the past. Guide me to always be light and to live unashamed, knowing you are the Master at using flawed and out-of-the-box people.

IV

TRIGGERS:

WHAT ARE YOUR TRIGGERS, AND HOW DO YOU MANAGE THEM?

I t was Friday the 13th. My husband Russ and I had only been married for a little over four months. Around the same time as our wedding, we sold our last renovated house, and we made the collective decision that I would write full-time, even if that meant being a one-income household for the foreseeable future. It was 11:00 am, and I was sitting in my little corner office (a.k.a. a desk in the corner of our master bedroom) while Kate was chatting with me from her favorite place on my grandma's cedar chest that sits at the end of our bed.

Russ works from home, and his office is in our finished basement. I don't know if it's because we live in a cabin or because our laundry room door is extremely loud when it closes, but I always hear him when he comes upstairs because he has to go through that door. Nothing seemed out of the ordinary to me when I heard the door shut and his footsteps in the kitchen.

Kate and I were still chatting as I heard the cupboard close, then another cupboard close, and finally, the refrigerator close in the background. All still seemed normal until Russ walked into the bedroom with one glass of wine and one of bourbon.

I looked at him, puzzled, laughed a little, looked at the clock again, and then jokingly said, "It's a little early, don't you think?" My husband, being the good-natured man that he is, smiled broadly and chuckled a little before saying, "Well, I have good news and bad news."

My stomach immediately felt like I was going down the biggest roller coaster hill ever.

I knew the company he worked for had been bought out by a much larger company out of Germany and that he was constantly stressed out about what that merger meant for the US branch he worked with. Before he could tell me anymore, my mind raced ahead a mile a minute, and I blurted out, "You got fired, didn't you?" Being the ever-patient human he is, he smiled and said, "I don't have to go to Germany next week – so that's the good news!"

That morning, when Russ got downstairs to his office and went to log in to his company accounts, he had no access. After pinging several other colleagues in the Americas, he quickly learned none of them had access either. In less than an hour, he learned that the Board had decided to disband the American Division of the Company. His boss in Germany didn't even know it was happening until right before Russ found out.

I am a planner. I am always five steps ahead. I don't fly by the seat of my pants. I like my world to be orderly, planned out, and predictable.

This was none of those things.

Even as Russ was talking to me, I couldn't stop the runaway train that my thoughts had apparently jumped on. I was working through each and every scenario in my mind – thinking about our budget, going over what we had in the savings, and figuring out how long Russ's severance would last while also making a mental list of all the things we needed to figure out. I had no idea how to get a job in this day and age, how much health insurance was going to cost, where Russ's resume was even stored, and when he last updated it.

The thing about my husband I adore is that he knows my brain works this way. Before he even came upstairs to tell me, he had already sat down at his computer with our budget, our bank account, and his severance package and figured out all the answers to these questions. Before I could even get them all out of my mouth, he started going over all of our details, and by the end of that conversation, I felt like I could breathe again.

That breathing lasted a few months.

Russ had been applying for jobs left and right during those few months, but he was only gaining minimal traction. When we both started to get discouraged, we put the job search on hold and did extensive research on the job market and interview process. We were even more overwhelmed after the research. This is a strange time of LinkedIn and Indeed, and software that scans your resume for keywords before a human even knows your name. There were so many profiles that had to be updated to look and sound a certain way and job listings that had to be scanned for keywords so those same keywords could then magically be insert-ed into different sections of Russ's resume. It felt like we were re-working his resume daily – sometimes multiple times a day – just to fit these different jobs that he was applying for.

As the months went on and he didn't find a job, I found my-self questioning what we were doing to make God withhold a job from Russ. I was so stressed out trying to determine what we had done to make God angry – did we need to tithe more? Were we not volunteering enough? Should we be serving more?

I spent about a week beating myself up over all the possibilities before I realized I had reverted to the years and years of bad theology that taught me that God would withhold blessings from me and punish me if I wasn't performing well enough or following the rules closely. Before this happened, I didn't even realize this was a trigger for me, but as soon as I identified it, I was able to work through it in a healthy way.

This one snuck up on me. It was like a tremor that kept running through my mind and disrupting my normal thought process. The tremors kept getting bigger and bigger until they finally transformed into a trigger, and I was able to identify what those tremors had been doing to me.

Even though I thought I was deep into my reconstruction process, these moments of being triggered made me realize that maybe I still had some work to do. While I had spent years deconstructing those key tenets of my faith, I realized there were other lingering ideas, teachings, and mindsets I didn't even know I needed to work through – and this was one of them.

BEING AWARE OF OUR TRIGGERS

It took me an entire week to be able to identify this trigger, and looking back on it now, I can even see that those seeds of doubt and the need to perform were nagging at me for several months before that. I knew an awareness of what triggered me during and after deconstruction and throughout the reconstruction process was paramount to my ability to overcome the cynicism, bitterness, and anger I had been harboring since the beginning of my journey. Through the experience with Russ's job, I learned that I'm still going to encounter triggers that I can't predict and even find myself blindsided by in the moment.

Like any trigger from any trauma, identifying the trigger was the first step to dismantling it and taking away its power. Once

I named it, I was able to work through all the feelings I had that were associated with that specific trigger. In this situation, those were feelings of guilt over the fact that we must not have been doing enough for God to bless us. Once I named those feelings, though, I was able to look at this situation logically and turn to truth instead of bad theology.

The reality of our situation wasn't that we weren't doing enough, tithing enough, serving enough, volunteering enough, or performing well enough. The reality was simply that Russ hadn't come across the right job for him yet. It was that simple. This wasn't a situation of God withholding blessing at all. As I finally worked through all my emotions and the logic behind the situation, my guilt turned to anger. I wasn't angry at the companies who weren't hiring my husband; I was angry at the institutions that had brainwashed me to believe that God would reward me according to my performance. I was angry that I had wasted so much of my life believing this about performance, stressing out about it, and then attempting to do everything I could to be good enough.

It took me a few months to work through my anger, sit in it, feel it, process it, and be able to move past it.

Months. Not hours, not days, but months. And you know what? That's okay. I needed that much time to sit with that trigger and the emotions from that trigger to be able to heal from the situations that created that trigger. The reality is that there have been other theological ideas that have triggered me, and for some of those, it has taken me years to process and heal. Some of them, I'm still healing from – they still make me angry, and I still have to work through that anger from time to time.

What I've learned about these triggers, though, is that I have to take the time to process them and then choose my response to them. I'm the only one who can do that. I might not have the power to redo my past, but I have the power to choose how I'm going to respond to it. And sometimes, still, I choose to be angry for a minute because it is righteous and justifiable anger.

One thing I try to never do when I'm triggered by something from my past is ignore it. I am not a compartmentalizer. I spent 38 years stuffing emotions and all the baggage that came with them into compartments in my heart, soul, mind – really anywhere I could shove them and not have to deal with them. Eventually, those doors holding all that baggage burst open. When they did, all the junk that had been shoved behind them came barreling out. And that was a scary, scary thing.

For those reasons, I don't shove emotions down or compartmentalize the things that trigger me. I sit with them. I analyze them. I break them down. I get to their core. You can ask Russ – it drives him crazy sometimes. I know myself well enough to know that if I don't work through them, they will end up haunting me later. That's what I would encourage you to do as well – sit with the things that trigger you, analyze them, break them down, and get to their core.

I have said it before, and I will say it again and again – there is no shame in therapy. You can love Jesus and your therapist! They are both amazing help in our times of trauma and trouble, but just because you have one doesn't mean you don't need the other. If this process of working through your triggers is something you need help with, there is no shame in working with a therapist.

RETHINKING THE THINGS THAT TRIGGER US

There's this cool thing that I've watched happen with those things that were my triggers. For some of those triggers, the process has been slow. For others, the process seems to happen in the blink of an eye. I'm an "aha moment" kind of person. Russ is one of those people who just gets things, while I'm someone who needs to put all the pieces together and connect all the dots before I see all the dots finally come together to complete the picture. That's the process I've seen happen again and again with my triggers.

I was sitting in church one Sunday. Jeff, one of our Pastors who also happens to have been my youth Pastor and is now one of my very best friends, was preaching about repentance. It was one of those Sundays when I saw the title of the sermon pop up on the screen after worship, and I immediately broke out into a cold sweat. Sometimes, I do this in church when I hear a topic that has been a trigger for me in the past, and I haven't worked through it all the way yet. Immediately, I knew this was going to be one of those days for me.

I started to think about why the topic of repentance would be a trigger for me, and my mind quickly connected to the fact that I had spent years in a church that never mentioned the word "grace." The focus was always on us, what we could and should do, instead of God and what He had already done for us. I remember sitting in that service through the first 10 minutes or so and honestly thinking I might have to leave the service if I didn't hear anything about grace quickly.

At about the time when I was thinking I was going to lose my mind in the middle of the church building, the entire direction of the sermon shifted from us to God, and I felt my heart rate begin to slow down again.

See, the thing about Jeff is that he escaped the same church I did. He has so much of the same church hurt and religious trauma as I do – plus some more of his own, as he wasn't just a member of that church but employed by them. He's worked for years to overcome bad theology, too. I know all of those things, and yet, I still almost had an anxiety attack waiting for him to finally get to grace.

But he did.

That's been the cool thing for me in this process of reconstruction – rewriting that terrible theology and sitting in the presence of those who have done the same thing. Even though there are still times when I find myself holding my breath and hoping for the best, I've found that, eventually, I arrive at that point where I can breathe again. God always provides me with the people and situations to help me work through and heal from those terrible theological triggers.

When I find myself having to hold my breath, the reality is that I can choose my reaction. I can leave. I have every right to leave, to remove myself from situations that don't serve me. Sometimes, that's what's necessary. Other times, when I can think logically about a topic and have healed enough from it, I can sit back and simply acknowledge that what I'm hearing is not what I believe – and that's okay, too. I can respectfully agree to disagree. Every situation and every trigger is different, though. Some triggers are too big for me to be able to respectfully disagree on, and those are the situations I choose to remove myself from.

An Ongoing Process

As I worked through my triggers and this process of reconstruction, one of the major theological aspects that I had to wrestle with was the idea of baptism. I was raised to believe that the only way to go to heaven was to be immersed in baptism. For years and years of my life, this was the teaching I received with plenty of cherry-picked Scripture passages to back those ideas up. When I started to cast off the theology of that church and read the Bible without their lens, baptism was a huge sticking point for me, and I made it my personal life goal to undo this damaging theology for as many people as I could.

We're twenty years into a church startup that sprung from the castoffs, outcasts, and misfits of the high-control church brotherhood I grew up in. It has only been in the last few years that I have sat back and listened to them talk about baptism in a way that is counter to the brainwashing I received. During this twentieth year, I sat and listened to the best sermon on baptism I've ever heard.

Even though I was at peace with my own beliefs on baptism, for the first time in my entire life, I was at peace with the theology and teachings of my church on baptism. I didn't think this would ever happen. I thought this would be one of those triggers and theological tenets that we would have to agree to disagree on, but I was wrong. And I've never been so happy to be wrong in my entire life.

I got a text from Jason after he preached the sermon saying it wasn't until he was writing it and doing a baptism that he realized he was smack dab in the middle of his own deconstruction/reconstruction moment. He explained how the wording he had always used during the ceremony of baptism was "for the forgiveness of sins and the gift of the Holy Spirit," but he realized that vernacular was a remnant of his past life that he needed to dismantle and rebuild.

More than anything, this text strand gave me hope. It made me realize I'm not alone, that I'm not the only one working through trauma and triggers from bad theology, and that the process for growth and healing can be an ongoing one for all of us – even our pastors.

JUST WHEN YOU THINK YOU'RE OVER IT...

There is no set timetable for healing, and acknowledging this process and that it takes time has been one of the most helpful aspects of my journey from deconstruction to reconstruction. It's also helped me immensely to understand that I might not ever work through every single trigger or religious trauma, but I want to have the tools to deal with them when I am triggered by something in the present that correlates to my past.

For me, it seems like every single time I think I've tackled the majority of my issues with religious trauma, something else rears its ugly head, and I find myself right back in that process of working through another trigger.

Since the beginning of my deconstruction journey, I've wholeheartedly known that one of my biggest frustrations is judgmental people who think they're "holier than thou." I've made the conscious choice to remove those types of people from my circle and my sphere of influence because I know that I just can't be with them. It isn't good for my mental or emotional health. They are one of those triggers I know I have to completely separate myself from because I just can't make myself agree to disagree and move on with them.

It isn't just those types of people, though. I recognize that same frustration when I listen to Christian radio, and there's quite a bit of talking between songs. The amount of Christianese, "holier-than-thou" mantras, and cringy verbiage that flows over the radio waves drives me insane, but sometimes I'm just too lazy to connect my phone and turn something else on, and country radio is the only other option out here in the sticks where I live. Innocently, one day, I was listening to Christian radio only for the music.

I got sucked in, though.

I'm one of those people who can tell you exactly where I was, what I was wearing, and who was with me etc., when certain impactful events happened in my life. This was one of those moments – all because of "holier-than-thou" judgmental radio show hosts on a local Christian radio station. They were talking about this app that uses AI to let you text back and forth with Jesus. At first, I laughed a little because I wasn't surprised that this is where our world has ended up. But then, they started talking about how you could choose other Bible folks to text with, and they noticed Judas was on the list.

The conversation quickly turned from this light-hearted discussion of this AI app to a full-on blastfest on Judas. One of them was explaining how they immediately clicked on that option to text with him, but they couldn't because it cost extra – it was only a premium feature. Then, for the next couple of minutes, they talked about how they would never pay to talk to Judas, how absurd that was, and how they could never understand why anyone would want to pay money to talk to Judas.

I was immediately triggered for a variety of reasons. My first thought was that they just alienated at least 50% of their audience who themselves are currently feeling like the Judas in their worlds. Then, I thought more about why I was angry and triggered, and I realized it was because this was the attitude of so many people in the church I grew up in – they ignored their sins and their own Judas moments to criticize and judge everyone else's. I was so triggered by five minutes of Christian radio because of the amount of judgment flowing over the airwaves that I chose to speak on it for the communion meditation in our church a few weeks later. Even though I thought I had healed from my years of life with judgmental people, that experience showed me I was wrong, and I still had some work to do in that area.

PROCESSING EMOTIONS LIKE DAVID

When I first began my deconstruction journey, I started in the Psalms. Honestly, I don't know why. I don't know why that is the first book that I thought I would read without the lens of my childhood church. I was blown away by David's honesty and the amount of times he prayed for his enemies to be destroyed. It literally made me laugh out loud and rethink prayer entirely. There was something about the rawness of David's prayers, his honesty about his weakness and failures, and his complete belief that God would be his rescuer that resonated with me in a way I had never experienced from church or church people before. As I read through all of his prayers and songs, I couldn't help but think about the sheer amount of emotion they were filled with.

David constantly poured out his heart – all of it – to God, and God still considered him a man after His own heart.

Even when David imploded his life several times over, he continued to pray with such raw, honest emotion. I think we can learn so much about processing our emotions that come from our triggers by reading the Psalms and approaching our emotions like David. Over and over again, David laments crisis after crisis after crisis and begs for deliverance from his enemies. For some of us, the church has become our enemy, and we could benefit from letting out our emotions in the same manner David did throughout the Psalms.

Maybe the next time you're triggered by something in the church or a faith community, you can let your emotions out through something similar to what David wrote in Psalm 5[22]:

SONG OF THE CLOUDED DAWN

For the Pure and Shining One
For her who receives the inheritance, by King David

MORNING WATCH

1 Listen, Yahweh, to my passionate prayer!
Can't you hear my groaning?
2 Don't you hear how I'm crying out to you?

---

[22] Psalm 5 TPT

My King and my God, consider my every word,
for I am calling out to you.
3 At each and every sunrise you will hear my voice
as I prepare my *sacrifice of* prayer to you.
Every morning I lay out the pieces of my life on the altar
and wait *for your fire to fall upon my heart.*

MAKING IT RIGHT

4 I know that you, God, are never pleased with lawlessness,
and evil ones will never be invited into your house.
5 Boasters collapse, unable to survive your scrutiny,
for your hatred of evildoers is clear.
6 You will make an end of all those who lie.
How you hate their hypocrisy and despise all who love violence!

MULTITUDE OF MERCY

7 But I know that you will welcome me into your house,
for I am covered by your covenant of mercy and love.
So I come to your sanctuary with deepest awe
to bow in worship and adore you.
8 Yahweh, lead me in the pathways of your pleasure
just like you promised me you would,
or else my enemies will conquer me.
Smooth out your road in front of me,
straight and level, so that I will know where to walk.

MULTITUDE OF SINS

9 Their words are unreliable.

Destruction is in their hearts,

drawing people into their darkness with their speeches.

They are smooth-tongued deceivers, flattering with their words.

10 Declare them guilty, O God!

Let their own schemes be their downfall!

Let the guilt of their sins collapse on top of them,

for they rebel against you.

MULTITUDE OF BLESSINGS

11 But let them all be glad,

those who turn aside to hide themselves in you.

May they keep shouting for joy forever!

Overshadow them in your presence as they sing and rejoice.

Then every lover of your name will burst forth with endless joy.

12 Lord, how wonderfully you bless the righteous.

Your favor wraps around each one and covers them

under your canopy of kindness and joy.

I love how David vents all of his emotions and how he lays it all out without holding anything back. But I also love how David processes his emotions, always brings his heart and mind back to what he knows is true, and then gives himself permission to move forward. I think that's what we have to remember and try to do when we're faced with triggers and all of the emotions that come with them.

IDENTIFYING AND WORKING THROUGH TRIGGERS ON YOUR RECONSTRUCTION JOURNEY

I wish I could have sat down at the beginning of my reconstruction journey and written a comprehensive list of all of my triggers, but that would have required me to know all of my triggers. I'm not too proud to admit that I didn't and still don't know all of them. I've accepted that there's a distinct possibility that I'm going to be working through triggers for the rest of my life. Now, though, I feel prepared to work through them as I continue this reconstruction process – which I've also accepted might be a lifelong process because I don't think I'm ever going to have all the answers. As you walk through this journey, let me encourage you to find a process for dealing with your triggers that works best for you and is healthiest for you.

If you need a place to start, this is the process that has worked for me:

1. *Identifying the Trigger:*
   Whether it's a giant, obvious trigger that immediately causes your body and brain to go into fight, flight, or freeze mode or a smaller trigger – like a tremor — that doesn't hit you all at once but creeps up on you over time, identifying and naming each of these triggers is important. Don't shove it down. Don't ignore it. Don't just hope it will pass. Call it by its name so you can begin to take its power.

2. *Identify your Feelings.*
   I grew up in the 80s and 90s when the most prominent parenting philosophy involved phrases like: "But, did anyone die? Is there blood? Suck it up and get over it." There wasn't much room for sitting with your feelings during those times. Consequently, it wasn't until I went through extensive therapy that I learned to feel my emotions, that

they were valid, and that I needed to honor them. These triggers from your church hurt and religious trauma will undoubtedly stir up emotion, and it very well could be emotion that has never been validated. Friend, your feelings are valid. Your responses to your trauma are valid. Give yourself the time to sit and identify those feelings and sit in them while you process the trigger and the emotion.

3. *Understand your Emotions*
Too often, we stop the process at simply identifying our feelings. Healing from religious trauma means moving beyond just acknowledging your feelings to understanding why it is you are feeling this way about this specific trigger. When I think back over all the different things that have been triggers for me, they have stirred up different emotions in me – sometimes it's fear, sometimes it's guilt, sometimes it's anger, sometimes it's frustration, and sometimes it's sadness. What I've learned is that if I can name what I'm feeling and then analyze why that particular trigger affected me in that manner, I can work through those emotions and heal, which allows me to continue moving forward and working on the hard job of reconstructing a healthy and whole faith.

4. *Choosing your Response*
There are very few things we have control over in this world, but the one thing we always have control over is ourselves, our responses, and our actions. The beauty of this is that we get to choose how we respond to our triggers. For me, there are some things I can't be around. When my life intersects with those things, I exit quietly. I don't throw a fit, make a scene, or put them on blast online (usually). I can choose to leave. I can choose to exit a conversation, a

church, a lecture, etc. I have the freedom to do that, and so do you. For other things, I can logically process the fact that I disagree, and that's okay. I don't have to shout from the rooftops that I disagree, but I can know in my heart and mind that what I'm hearing is not my position and that other people are entitled to their opinions as well. It's the tremors I can deal with more than the triggers, though – the ideas or opinions that aren't hurting other people but that have some connection to my past.

Just because these are the responses that work the best for me does not mean that they are the responses that will always work best for you. You might be in a situation where responding to a trigger might mean you need to have a conversation with someone from your past or present. Your responses might mean completely cutting yourself off from certain individuals who have been integral parts of your life. Your responses might mean keeping a journal or creating a blog where you can address your triggers, traumas, and the religious harm in your life.

If you are struggling with this part of your reconstruction journey, I will once again encourage you to seek out a licensed therapist who has experience working with survivors of religious trauma and spiritual abuse. There are so many quality therapists out there, and it seems like every day there are more and more therapists who specialize in helping people who have been victims of religious trauma and abuse.

Friends, you're probably sick of hearing me say this is hard work, but it's worthy work. I can't emphasize this enough. Acknowledging your triggers, understanding your emotions, and choosing your response is hard work, but it is worthy work!

REFLECTIONS: TRIGGERS

Remember:

- Some triggers start out as tremors.
- Compartmentalizing and ignoring triggers is not healthy.
- Everyone's triggers are different.
- Naming a trigger is the first step to taking its power away.
- You might not ever know all of your triggers.
- Healing from your triggers is a hard process.
- The one thing you can control is how you respond to triggers.
- Identifying triggers and why they're your triggers helps eliminate the anger, bitterness, and sadness on your reconstruction journey.

Receive:

Psalm 7 TPT

Song for the Slandered Soul

> *David's passionate song to Yahweh*
>
> *To the tune of "Breaking the Curse of Cush, the Benjamite"*

Rescue Me

> 1 Yahweh, my God, I turn to hide my soul in you.
>
> Save me from all those who pursue and persecute me.
>
> 2 There is none to deliver me *but you!*
>
> Don't let my foes fall upon me like fierce lions with teeth bared.
>
> Can't you see how they want to rip my soul to shreds?
>
> 3 Yahweh, my God, if I have done evil like they say I have,
>
> and my hands are guilty,
>
> 4 if I have wronged someone at peace with me,
>
> if I have betrayed a friend, repaying evil for good,
>
> or if I have unjustly harmed my enemy,

5 *Then* let my enemy pursue and overtake me.

Let them grind me into the ground.

Let them take my life from me and drag my dignity through the dust!

Pause in his presence

Vindicate Me

6 Yahweh, arise in your anger against the anger of my enemies.

Awaken your fury and stand up for me!

Execute the judgment you have decreed against them.

7 All the people gather around you.

Return to your place on high to preside over them.

8 You are Yahweh who judges the people.

Vindicate me *publicly*, Yahweh, and restore my honor and integrity.

Declare me innocent.

9 Once and for all, bring to an end the evil tactics of the wicked!

Establish the *cause of* the righteous,

for you are the righteous God, *the soul searcher*,

who tests every heart

to examine the thoughts and motives.

10 God, your wraparound presence is my shield.

You bring victory to all who are pure in heart.

11 God, your righteousness is revealed when you judge.

Because of the strength of your forgiveness,

your anger does not break out every day.

God's Lethal Weapons

12-13 Yet if one does not repent,
you will not relent to sharpen your *shining* sword.
You have an arsenal of lethal weapons
that you've prepared for them.
You have bent and strung your bow,
making your judgment-arrows shafts of burning fire.
14 Look how the wicked conceive their evil schemes.
They go into labor with their lies and give birth to trouble.
15 They dig a pit *for others to fall into*,
not knowing that they will be the very ones
who will fall into it.
16 Every pit-digger who works to trap and harm others
will be trapped by his own treachery.

Thankful Praise

17 But I will give my thanks to you, Yahweh,
for you make everything right in the end.
I will sing my highest praise to the God of the Highest Place!

Reflect:

1. Spend some time writing out the different things you know
are triggers for you. Start a list in a journal and give yourself
room to come back and reflect on each one of them.
2. For each trigger, take a few minutes to think about what
emotions they evoke in you. Write down the emotion next
to each trigger.
3. For each emotion, take a few minutes to think about where
that emotion comes from. Write it down.

4. For each trigger, think about a strategy for how you will respond when faced with that trigger next. What do you need to do for yourself that is healthy? Leave? Discuss? Agree to Disagree? Something else entirely?

5. Write a prayer that mirrors David's structure in the psalms. Don't hold anything back. Be honest about what you are feeling, why you are feeling that way, and what you need God to do for you to help you deal with these emotions and this trigger.

Prayer:

God, I know that there are things in my life that are triggers for me. I know that they stem from my past and the ways I have been hurt by the church or dealt with religious trauma. God, I give those triggers to you. I pray that as I face them in the future, you would help me to see them, to pause and sit in my emotions, to understand why I feel the way, and to choose my response in a healthy manner. God, I commit to honesty with you. I commit to praying like David, to not holding back my heart from you, and to seeking only truth in you and in my prayer and spiritual life.

V

ALL THE FEELS:
ALLOWING YOURSELF TO FEEL
YOUR EMOTIONS

It was just a normal Sunday morning. I had donned my dress clothes, as I always did on Sunday mornings, and headed to the small-ish country church in "middle-of-nowhere" Ohio. I walked into the brand new "sanctinasium" where services were held on Sundays and Wednesdays, but basketball leagues were held during the week.

As soon as I walked into the building, the charged energy smacked me in the face. There seemed to be some electric undercurrent running through the congregation that I couldn't pinpoint. I knew, though, that something wasn't right.

The people I had spent years worshiping and serving with were avoiding eye contact with me and my family. The usual happy, shiny smiles had been replaced with forced almost-smiles, the usual chit chat and talk about the weather replaced with silence.

As the service began, nothing seemed amiss, and throughout the service, all seemed to follow the prescribed and typical plan. As the service came to a close, one of the elders took the mic. He explained that the elders and deacons who were up for renewal would be voted at the conclusion of the service. Then, he directed anyone who was not a member of the church to leave the sanctuary.

As the visitors took their leave, deacons went from row to row, passing out ballots. I saw it then. My dad's name was on the ballot. Next to his name were two options: yay or nay. In that moment, I realized why the energy had seemed charged, why the people who had known me forever were distant, and why there was a cloak of doom hovering around the service.

These people were preparing to vote my dad out of leadership.

I was in my early twenties and still under the false impression that I knew everything about everything and had all of the answers to all of life's burning questions. I hadn't quite arrived at the point in life where you realize that you actually don't know much in the grand scheme of things and that what you know today might change tomorrow because life is like that.

I was attending and serving in the church I grew up in. Previously, my family attended the tiny country church my mom grew up in. We switched churches when I was in 4th grade, and my brother was in 7th grade. They wanted more for us, and since my brother was in Junior High, they were looking for a church that had a youth group for him. The churches were only 15 minutes away from each other, but there might as well have been an entire world between them in terms of size, programs, and people. The theology was the same, though, so the only major change I saw in my life at that time in terms of teaching was that the humble Sunday School teachings of Dorothy Underwood were replaced with much more patriarchal teachings by men.

Within just a few years of being at the new church, my dad became a deacon and eventually an elder. At that point in my twenties, I couldn't even remember a time when my dad wasn't in a leadership position in the church. The late 90s and early 2000s were strange times in churches. These were decades of change in non-denominational churches where the shift was happening from hymns to choruses and from hymnals to overhead projectors.

Those changes didn't come easily in many of the smaller, rural churches in our area. At the time, the church I attended was considered progressive by many of the other churches in our brotherhood because we didn't just have an overhead projector; we had a praise team, too. Sometimes, we even had a guitar player! While some people were cheering on change, others were adamantly against it–insistent that choruses were "devil music" and guitars had no place in worship services.

As the church continued to evolve, attendance continued to increase, and with that increase in attendance came an increase in giving. As the seats became fuller and fuller every Sunday, it became obvious that we had to do something differently to fit all the new people.

The solution to the people problem was a combination of multiple services and the launch of a building campaign. Naively, I thought the constant conflict between the old and new would dissipate once we had a new building. I was wrong. Instead of the conflict dissipating, it blew up. There was a sect of people who wanted things to go back to the way they had always been done – so much so that they actually wanted to move back into the old building – except they couldn't move back into the old building because the pews from the old building had been sold and it had been turned into a youth building.

Sunday mornings became a constant balancing act as everyone did their best to try to keep everyone happy and not rock the boat too much. Meanwhile, this was also during the boom of home groups and small groups. As an elder, my dad led one of these home groups, and his group was full of people who were constantly looking to the future, seeking change, and attempting to hear God's voice amid the chaos.

The folks who were hellbent on returning to the old traditions of the church did not like this one bit. They staged a coup. When the time came for the congregational vote for the elders and deacons, this group went behind my dad's back and campaigned to have him and the one other elder seeking God's voice and progress out of leadership.

It was such a weird time. We felt betrayed–like we had lost an integral part of our lives and something we had held dear for so long. Not only that, but we lost our community, our friends, and the people who had played all the roles in our lives for decades. With one vote, we lost everything because those people who had campaigned against my dad were the same people who supposedly loved us and supported us. They came to our baptisms, launched us into the world at our graduations, made up our wedding parties, and visited us in the hospital. These were supposed to be our people.

Just like that, they were gone, and we had no idea what would come next. I had attended a Christian college from a different denomination, and they had several thriving churches in our area. For a few months, we attended those on Sunday mornings, feeling numb. It was all so surreal and impossible to comprehend. Even attending those churches on Sunday mornings, we never felt like anything more than visitors because we hadn't yet accepted that we were spiritually homeless at that point.

After several months passed and we still hadn't found a church home, the shame set in. Up until that point, I had spent the entirety of my life believing my church and its sister churches were right and everyone else was wrong. There I was, sitting in one of those other churches from a different denomination every Sunday morning, wondering if I had been wrong for all of those years or if these people who seemed to wholeheartedly love Jesus were wrong and were actually going to hell – like I had been taught. Even though it was completely irrational, I felt so guilty because it felt like I was betraying the church and the belief system I had dedicated my entire life to – even though it had just completely betrayed me. I couldn't find a way to make my heart and mind reconcile what had happened with what I believed. In fact, there was a time following this betrayal that I thought we should find another church in our brotherhood to attend because I thought that would help me reconcile my feelings.

There were a couple of problems with that line of thinking, though. The first problem was that I was already starting to silently question some of the teachings of the church because of how they wielded their (flawed) theology against my dad. I didn't dare say anything out loud about it because I was afraid I would be labeled a heretic, but the seed had been planted. The other problem was that once you get voted out of leadership at one of these churches, you're blackballed. So, planting ourselves in another similar congregation wasn't really an option unless we wanted to be the outcasts.

I would never have chosen for my family to go through this experience. I see now how being burned so severely by the church I grew up in burst my heart wide open to receive the truth I didn't even know I needed. It didn't take long for me to start questioning the theology I had been raised with and to understand that other denominations were not, in fact, sending their members straight to hell. In some ways, that realization was more difficult for me to accept than the betrayal by our church family. To accept this belief as truth logically meant I had to consider the errancy of everything else I had been taught as well. The thought nagged at the back of my mind for years and years while I matured enough to gain the tools I needed to meticulously deconstruct those thoughts.

NEW LIFE

After we got blackballed from my childhood church and then spent months at another denomination, something exceptionally unexpected sprung to life. There was a group of individuals who loved Jesus but who had been completely burned by the brotherhood of churches we had been kicked out of. They felt God nudging them to do church differently. They talked extensively about who God is and what church should look like, and they launched a church a mere 10 miles from our old church.

This might come as a shock to some of you, but it's still the church I attend today. It's the church I served in before I imploded my life, the church I healed in as I faced the consequences of my terrible decisions, the church that visited me, sent me cards and emails, and loved me while I was in prison, and the church where I sat for five years on Sunday mornings after prison to heal. Now, it's the church I serve in, the place I call home, and where I learned to breathe again.

Because I was there from the beginning, watched it form from the ground up, and loved and trusted the leadership, I didn't continue to question the theology I grew up with. Instead, I was just glad to be out of that environment and in a church that wasn't full of toxicity and harm. Now that I'm through the deconstruction process and working through the reconstruction process, I speak loudly, openly, and without hesitation about my experiences. Here's what I've learned: everyone in leadership at my church has gone through their own deconstruction journey, is still working on their reconstruction journey, and didn't have the language to verbalize it at first.

Imploding my life in a very public way changed me in so many ways. This might seem strange to some of you, but there is a freedom that comes with the entire world knowing the worst thing you've ever done. Honestly, it makes everything else in your life pale in comparison. After I worked through the embarrassment, shame, and consequences of my self-destruction with the help of good friends, godly mentors, and licensed therapists, I became a much more authentic version of myself. I had no more need for masks, no need for pedestals or podiums, and no need to perform a certain way to meet people's expectations for fear of disappointing them. I could be unabashedly myself. And with that realization came the open discussion of my deconstruction, the damage of the flawed and toxic theology I grew up with, and the transparency of my struggles and wrestling with God.

When those situations happen, we have a choice to turn to God or to turn away from Him. I never saw it as an option to turn away from God during the devastation because I saw God as my only lifeline through the hell I had to endure. As much as I hate saying it (because I recognize how terrible my mistake was), I know I wouldn't be who I am today without all of those experiences. I know God has taken my terrible decisions and these things that should have destroyed me, and He has redeemed them. He consistently uses them for so much good in my own life and the lives of those He intersects me with. So, while I wish this growth and those intersections would have happened differently, I can't deny the growth that's come from them. I'm forever grateful for the shift that happened from a quiet deconstruction to a very loud reconstruction within my circle and faith community.

You would think that after such a traumatic betrayal and "come to Jesus moment" (see what I did there?), I would have immediately worked to deconstruct all the other faulty theological teachings I had been raised with, but it didn't work that way for me. I've thought about this so much – how the environment was perfect for a complete deconstruction and reconstruction – but as I look back on my life and my heart, I recognize the fact that I just wasn't ready yet.

When I finally was ready, though, the deconstruction happened quietly, but the reconstruction happened loudly because once I accepted that I needed it, I was outraged and felt like I needed to shout it from the mountaintops.

THE PRODIGAL CHILD

With that very loud reconstruction came all sorts of feelings I wasn't prepared for. My extended family is tight-knit. My mom and her sister married cousins, resulting in a couple of things: first, it looks like my family tree doesn't branch because everyone on both sides of my family has the same last name, but second, it doesn't feel like I have two sides to my family because everyone knows everyone and is somehow related in multiple ways to each other. Until my daughter Kate was 14, she wondered why we never saw my mom's side of the family because everyone had my dad's last name. Oops.

My family is so tight-knit that while I was growing up, we all went to the same type of churches even though we didn't go to the same church– until we got kicked out. Even then, after the new church was started, everyone accepted that we might not be going to hell because our new church was non-denominational. We have a rather large Thanksgiving dinner with all of this extended family. On what we refer to as "the big year," there are around 40 of us, but even on "the small year," there are still 25 of us. It wasn't until a couple of years after my giant deconstruction journey that I started to loudly and publicly reconstruct. I didn't think anything of my very public writings criticizing the faulty theology of my church – the church some of my extended family still attends – until that first Thanksgiving, at which time I panicked.

Like every other family, we have all sorts of closets with skeletons in them. I knew this, and I've found out more since. But despite all those skeletons and all those closets, the one thing my family has going for it is that everyone has somewhat similar theological beliefs. I survived all of the Thanksgivings that followed the implosion of my life, but I was dreading the first one following my public reconstruction like I dreaded the flu for one reason (and maybe it's one that you can relate to): I didn't want to be seen as a prodigal child.

Deconstruction has such a negative connotation in many faith circles, including my former one. I knew if my family members who were still active in that faith community knew I was deconstructing, they would view me as the prodigal who had left the faith. I didn't see myself as a prodigal child at all during my deconstruction/reconstruction journey, though. I was simply someone who was purposefully seeking truth and answers. I wasn't trying to squander my inheritance, but I feared those family members who were still involved in the type of church I grew up in wouldn't see it that way at all. I didn't want to have to spend my Thanksgiving fielding the looks of pity from my well-meaning family members or defending my reconstructed belief system. I had so many feelings related to all of this that I couldn't even keep track of all of them because they were constantly in conflict with each other – the fear, guilt, and shame on one hand versus the freedom, pride, and confidence on the other.

QUIET DECONSTRUCTION AND LOUD RECONSTRUCTION

What I didn't know or understand at the time was the emotions that I was feeling were valid, and the majority of them were connected to the stages of grief. If you aren't familiar with the stages of grief, they were created as a model for how the terminally ill approach and deal with their death by Elisabeth Kubler-Ross. They became more widely known and gained popularity after she published her book *On Death and Dying* in 1969. Over time, Kubler-Ross's model has been adapted more generally to different types of grief.

Even though I didn't realize it was grief at first, I was grieving the loss of something that had been an integral part of my life and my identity. It took time for me to understand I had to go through the grieving process and that it would take time. While I didn't understand what was happening with my emotions at the time, I hope it can be different for you. I hope you can work to understand the stages of grief and see how you are working through them as you mourn what you lost and begin to reconstruct your future because these are important in the healing process.

While people tend to think these stages occur in a particular order, often, that isn't the case. In fact, it's not uncommon for individuals to go back and forth from stage to stage, to find themselves hanging out for a long time in a particular stage, or even to skip stages altogether.

Loneliness:
This isn't one of the stages of grief you'll find in all the textbooks, but from my experiences with grief, it is pervasive throughout various stages in the process. So, I'm taking the liberty of adding it here. When you walk away from a church, faith, or faith community, it can feel exceptionally lonely. For me, I walked away from the people and relationships that had sustained every aspect of my life for twenty-plus years. Before the betrayal, I would have told anyone who would have listened how these were my people, how they were like family to me, and how they

always had my back. To watch that evaporate right before my eyes was hard, and it was lonely. I was fortunate that several of our good friends were also voted out at the same time or left the church as a result of that vote soon after, but it still felt very lonely. My family wasn't the "just show up on Sunday Mornings" type of family. No, we were one of those families who were at the church building every time the church doors opened. So, not only did it feel lonely because we had lost so many relationships, but it also felt lonely because we didn't know how to fill our time.

You might be experiencing this loneliness right now, too. Whether you recently left a faith community or you've been gone for some time, you undoubtedly have a hole that community once filled. Likely, you lost friends, and maybe even loved ones, when you left who you thought would be in your life forever.

Denial

The definition of *denial* in terms of the stages of grief relates to the feeling of numbness that comes after death or loss. It's that period where we haven't accepted who or what we've lost completely, and we tend to walk around as if nothing has happened. Even though we logically know in our heads that we've lost something, our hearts don't want to accept it.

Even as I sit here today, years later, reflecting on my journey, I'm still struck by the different times I swam around in the denial stage – some of those times were brief, but other times, I spent years there.

When we were first kicked out of the church I grew up in, this stage was brief for me. While it took a minute for it to sink in that we had been blackballed, the numbness that followed was short. It was quickly replaced with all sorts of other emotions: anger, anxiety, and fear, mainly. It was different for me when I deconstructed, though. It took me years to acknowledge that I needed to deconstruct and then reconstruct – decades even. For those decades after I left my childhood church and before I did the hard work of deconstruction and reconstruction, I was just living in this denial stage. I was numb all the time, and while there was this subconscious feeling deep in my soul that I had lost something, I wasn't able to put my finger on it, grab ahold of it, and pull it loose.

While everyone is different and none of our journeys look identical, for most of us, I think the denial stage of grief tends to happen early on – possibly at the very beginning stages of the journey. For most of us working toward reconstruction, we have probably already worked through this stage, even if we did it unknowingly. However, you might find yourself in denial right now, not understanding how you got to this point and not wanting to think this is the reality of the rest of your life.

Do you remember when you first started to have those thoughts that maybe something was amiss in your church or your belief system, but you couldn't put your finger on what it was exactly? Maybe, too, it was that time when you knew precisely what was wrong, but you didn't want to accept it as your reality. Then, even when you started to see reality, you found ways to talk yourself out of believing it. This is where I found myself for years. Even after we were kicked out of our church, there were years there when I still felt like the church had positives and truth, and we would find another church that aligned with those beliefs.

I refused to accept the fact that we had literally been kicked out of the brotherhood and that there were some inherent problems at work within the theology of the church.

For most people, this stage happens before they ever really accept or acknowledge that they're deconstructing, and maybe that's how it happened for you. For others, it happens during that time of deconstruction when you have left or are in the process of leaving. You find yourself struggling to feel anything or to accept that this part of your life is dying even when you logically know the truth in your head. Your heart struggles to get on the same page with your head.

Anger

Anger is such a common emotion to feel when something or someone has died. Loss can feel unfair. It can feel cruel, like the world is out to get you, or even like Satan is targeting you. It can feel like you are witnessing the loss of your future and all of your plans, and that is unsettling. When we deal with the loss of a person, we have someone to grieve, but when we deal with the loss of theology, a church, or our faith, it can be disconcerting and disheartening. For many of us, we are grieving the death of a set of beliefs or a community that has been part of our lives forever. We find ourselves angry at the system, at individuals, at the church, and maybe even at our families for their role in establishing our belief system.

Not only did I spend copious amounts of time camping out with my anger, but I still find myself here in the anger stage over and over again. When I stumble across a new trigger, I still get angry – angry at the system and angry at the people who perpetrated the system. If I'm being completely honest, I think I was angry throughout the majority of my deconstruction journey. As I continued to read the Bible without the lens of my previous church, so many glaring inconsistencies in their theology jumped out at me, and each time I found something new, I would get fired up. I didn't understand how they had continued to preach their faulty theology for so many years without more people seeing how messed up it was.

It wasn't just the system or the church that I was angry at, though. I spent a significant amount of time angry at myself for falling prey to their theology, for not reading the Bible without their lens years before, for not listening to my gut when it was telling me how contradictory these teachings were, for arguing with Embrey when I was in elementary school, for dedicating my life to rules, regulations, and performance instead of understanding grace and the goodness of God.

If I'm being completely transparent, it still makes me angry.

As someone who has always been considered "smart" and "logical," my ego took a giant hit when I came face to face with the fact that I had allowed myself to be completely misled for the entirety of my life. That made me so disappointed and angry with myself.

Your experiences with anger toward the system, a church, and people in the church might look different than mine, but when you find yourself experiencing it, I hope you acknowledge and sit in it long enough to work through it. What I needed someone to say to me when I was deconstructing and what I consistently remind myself of now that I'm reconstructing is that my anger is valid. I have the right to be angry at this system, and I have a right to be angry at the people who perpetuated this system. What I have to remember when it comes to my anger with myself is that I'm human, and I have to give myself a bit of grace moving forward. The past is the past. I was young. I was following the traditions and the belief system of my family, and I had no reason to believe it was leading me astray when I was a little girl.

Bargaining

After we face loss, it's common for us to struggle to accept the fact that there is nothing we can do to regain what we have lost. During the bargaining stage of grief, we tend to want to "fix" things. We find ourselves bargaining with God, attempting to assess and adjust our behavior in hopes that things will turn out differently, and hoping that through some effort, we might have the power to change the course of our past and future.

This is also a time when we might find ourselves completely stuck in our heads. We keep replaying past scenarios and conversations, trying to figure out exactly where things went wrong. We might find ourselves asking a ton of those "what-if" questions and thinking about how if we had just thought a little differently, stood up to someone a little earlier, or listened to our gut a little better, we might not be in this situation at all.

For me, my anger and bargaining stages overlapped for a hot minute. I kept replaying situations, thinking about terrible sermons, asking myself, "What if I had done something differently there instead of mindlessly following?" This stage was hard for me. I beat myself up repeatedly and failed miserably at showing myself any grace.

Are you stuck in this stage? This is one of those places we can find ourselves camping out in for a very long time. Of all the stages of grief, moving through and beyond this one is paramount to your reconstruction journey.

You have to stop beating yourself up today, friend.

The beauty of reconstruction is in the freedom that comes from breathing freely in the presence of God without the heavy weight of high-control religion, toxic theology, and church hurt. You can't experience that freedom and those easy breaths if the weight of your past is sitting heavily on your shoulders and your chest.

Today has to be the day when you say goodbye to the guilt, stop replaying the past, and quit believing that if you act or perform a certain way, God is going to love you more.

Depression

When we think about grieving a loss, one of the first things that likely comes to mind is sadness. We might even feel like our lives have lost their meaning when we lose someone or something important to us. Just like the bargaining stage of grief, the depression stage is also one we can find ourselves stuck in for quite some time, especially if we have left a faith, church, or high-control religion where our value and purpose were completely tied to our active participation.

It can feel like you are a ship without an anchor getting tossed around the ocean in the middle of a hurricane.

I don't want you to live there.

I want you to experience the freedom you were meant to have in Christ, but you can't do that if you stay on that ship in the middle of the ocean. Let God take you to the shore, jump off that ship, and place your feet on solid ground by being brave enough to sit with and feel the sadness, the hurt, and the depression for a time and then release it. If you are struggling to work through these emotions on your own, seek professional help from a trained professional who can help you process these feelings. Many folks who go through the deconstruction process find themselves morphing between the bargaining and depression stages, but they never move on from those. They've torn the house down, but they aren't rebuilding it. I want you to rebuild a house you can live in forever, and that's what the reconstruction process can do for you after you move away from this depression stage.

Acceptance

For many people, grief can be so fluid that it moves through every part of their lives. When we first lose something or someone, it can feel like the world will never be right again. For most people, though, over time, those feelings of hopelessness and depression dissipate. They might not disappear completely, but they lessen to a point where they become manageable. With that lessening comes a new normal. While there is still hurt related to who or what was lost, there is an acceptance of the loss, and I'm not sure you can ever truly move into a place of healthy reconstruction without the acceptance of what was lost.

For many of us who are staring down reconstruction and taking it on, that means accepting the loss of theology, faith communities, people we held dear and a life we thought we would have forever. And goodness, those are some heavy losses. Remember the story I told in the introduction about our hoarder house? When we completed it, it looked like a brand new beautiful house on the outside, but underneath all the new, the foundation was still there holding it all together. The completed renovation could have never coexisted with the hoarder house. One had to be dismantled completely before the new house could emerge. While the bones were still there, the detrimental parts were removed.

Your faith is no different. The bones are still there, but the detrimental parts have been removed to leave room for the beautiful masterpiece to be built. You might not be to this point of acceptance yet, but I pray that as you work through this journey and as you continue to share in these experiences with me, you can get there, too.

The reconstruction journey is a process, and it involves grieving what we've lost. In order to grieve what we've lost, we have to be willing to acknowledge the loss and the emotions that came with that loss. My prayer for you today, friend, is that you take the time you need to sit with those emotions, that you feel each and every one for as long as you need to so that you can heal and arrive at the point of acceptance if you aren't already at that point.

REFLECTIONS: ALL THE FEELS

Remember:

- Everyone's deconstruction/reconstruction journey is different.
- You might have multiple experiences in your life that contributed to your deconstruction/reconstruction.
- Leaving a church, faith community, theology, etc., is a loss.
- We have to grieve our losses.
- There are five stages of grief, and they aren't always linear.
- Loneliness is a part of grief.
- Your feelings are valid.
- Working through the stages of grief is an important part of the reconstruction journey.

Receive:

Romans 8:35-39 TPT:

Who could ever divorce us from the endless love of God's Anointed One? *Absolutely no one!* For nothing in the universe has the power to diminish his love toward us. Troubles, pressures, and problems are unable to come between us and heaven's love. What about persecutions, deprivations, dangers, and death threats? No, for they are all impotent to hinder omnipotent love, even though it is written:

All day long we face death threats for your sake, God.

We are considered to be nothing more

than sheep to be slaughtered!

Yet even in the midst of all these things, we triumph over them all, for God has made us to be more than conquerors, and his demonstrated love is our glorious victory over everything!

So now I live with the confidence that there is nothing in the universe with the power to separate us from God's love. I'm convinced that his love will triumph over death, life's troubles, fallen angels, or dark rulers in the heavens. There is nothing in our present or future circumstances that can weaken his love. There is no power above us or beneath us—no power that could ever be found in the universe that can distance us from God's passionate love, which is lavished upon us through our Lord Jesus, the Anointed One!

Reflect:

1. Take a few days to reflect on your deconstruction process. What was it like? What were the hardest parts about it?
2. What stage of grief are you in right now? If you aren't in the acceptance stage, what steps can you take to move toward acceptance?
3. What have the stages of grief looked like for you on this journey so far?
4. What are your biggest challenges as you work toward reconstructing your faith?
5. Spend a few minutes writing out what feelings you've experienced on this journey so far and reminding yourself that those feelings are valid.
6. Now that you've identified and processed your feelings and understood that they are valid, what are your goals for your reconstruction journey?

Prayer:

God, I recognize that the deconstruction/reconstruction journey is a long, difficult one. Even though I know that you love me unconditionally and are cheering me on in this journey, help me to feel your love and acceptance regardless of where I am on the journey and what stage of grief I'm in. Help me to see the stages of my grief with clarity and allow your hand to guide me toward acceptance.

VI

WHAT MATTERS MOST:
IDENTIFYING YOUR PRIORITIES AND GOALS FOR RECONSTRUCTION

I t was a random weekday evening, and we were sitting in my best friend Missy's living room. Her husband was at work because he worked 2nd shift those days, and her 7-year-old was playing in her bedroom. It had been an especially daunting week dealing with my divorce nonsense that only Missy could understand out of all my friends.

She looked at me like she always looked at me – with honesty, empathy, and sincerity — and said, "Kristen, you spent the first 38 years of your life being fine and telling everyone that everything was fine. No matter what was happening in your life or the lives of those around you, you were always fine. You've never asked for help. You've never been anything other than 'fine.' But now, now you're a totally different person."

Her words hit like a hammer straight to my soul.

She was right. I had spent 38 years of my life telling everyone that I was fine and that everything was fine even though I wasn't, and everything was far from it. There was something woven into my upbringing in the church that led me to believe that feeling my feelings and expressing those feelings equated to a moral failure. I was taught this failure was a weakness that resulted from my inability to perform how I was supposed to perform and signaled a separation from God and his disappointment in me.

For the record, that is faulty theology.

I didn't see it as faulty theology at the time, though. I saw it as absolute truth, one of the absolute truths that drove my decisions, actions, and life. It wasn't until I imploded my life and began deconstructing my faith that I recognized the lies involved in this line of thinking and how detrimental it was to my mental and emotional health. I can proudly say I have not once been "fine" since this conversation.

In this conversation with my friend and through the acceptance of the unconditional love of God, I shifted my perspective and attitude from one of performance to one of authenticity and transparency. I've learned that it is non-negotiable when it comes to my journey of reconstruction.

NOTHING CAN SEPARATE YOU FROM THE LOVE OF GOD

Two major shifts happened in my life as a result of that conversation: I realized that I don't always have to be fine or okay, and I don't always have to have the answer. There was a freedom and an openness that came with being authentic and transparent with my emotions. I quit saying I was fine and admitted how I felt when people asked me. If life was sucking at the moment, I never hesitated to say that. Admitting how my life was going opened the door for others to be authentic and transparent about how they were doing. I find myself looking people in the eye and telling them it's okay to say things suck right now, and if we're being honest, there are periods throughout this journey of reconstruction where things just suck.

The unexpected result of my authenticity and transparency was the freedom to abandon the belief that I had to have all the answers and always be right. See, growing up, the church taught me that I not only had to have all the answers all the time but also what the answers had to be. That was a hard mindset for me to abandon because I spent years believing that having all the answers and performing a certain way as a result of those answers is what made me a "good Christian." Even more than that, those things are what determined God's love for me. Even though they preached that God's love is unconditional, their theology taught the exact opposite. It taught me that I had to know specific things and act a certain way for God to love me, and if I didn't, God would punish or discipline me to get me back in line. Honestly, it makes me shudder to even write these words on paper.

Let me be very clear about this today: There is nothing you can do that can separate you from the love of God, and regardless of what you do, God's mercies are new every morning because he is faithful and just, and he will complete the good work he started in you.[23]

Mic drop.

Let me say that one more time and a little louder for those in the back: there is nothing you can do that will separate you from the love of God.

- Your deconstruction and reconstruction can not separate you from the love of God.
- The cult you were in cannot separate you from the love of God.

---
[23] Philippians 1:6

- Your questions cannot separate you from the love of God.
- Your doubt cannot separate you from the love of God.
- Your wrong answers cannot separate you from the love of God.
- Not attending church cannot separate you from the love of God.
- Your rebellion cannot separate you from the love of God.
- Nothing.
- Nothing can separate you from the love of God.

There are no asterisks, friend. You don't have to have all the answers, and nothing can separate you from the love of God.

I didn't understand this truth in my first 38 years. I don't think it really all sunk in with me until Kate got to the age where she started asking questions about church, God, and theology. I remember one of my most foundational conversations with her about church and theology. She had been to church with some of her family members. They wanted her to bow her head and close her eyes during prayer, and she didn't understand why that was because that wasn't how we taught her to approach prayer.

Looking back, my fight-or-flight response kicked in because I immediately nipped this idea of having to close her eyes during prayer in the bud and was adamant that she pray however she felt she needed to. At that moment, I realized how terrified I was that she would suffer in the church the same way I had, and my main priority was to break that cycle.

I never wanted her to feel like God was going to love her any less. I wanted her to always be wrapped in the unconditional love of God in a way I only began to understand as an adult. My sole goal was to make sure she understood this unconditional love. She didn't need to bow her head and close her eyes to get God's attention. She could talk to Him however she was comfortable.

After that conversation, I realized that I was responsible for ensuring she continued to understand that God wouldn't love her any less when she didn't have all the answers and that she never had to be "fine." I began to make sure she understood the truth about all the things I was misled by in the church throughout my life–that she had her own identity, she wasn't broken, and she could "just say no" to the lies of purity culture. We talked, and still talk, at length about Jesus's discussion with the disciples at the Last Supper about the call to love God and love people, and how that should be our primary goal as Christ-followers.

Those are the things that matter, and those are the things I've recognized shaped my faith as I reconstructed it, but without the Spirit using Missy and Kate to nudge me toward understanding, I never would have understood them.

PERSONAL VS. CORPORATE FAITH

There was this really strange dichotomy in my childhood church that I carried with me long into adulthood, and I've struggled to dismantle it over the years. I was raised with the words from the pulpit and those of Sunday School teachers being that I needed to have a personal relationship with God. Conversely, I was also taught from the same pulpits and from those same teachers that I needed to follow a certain set of rules, perform in a certain way, and meet certain expectations to be loved, accepted, and remain in God's family.

Many of those expectations revolved around what I was sup-posed to believe and experience in the church, as well as those things I was specifically taught I was never to experience because they didn't exist in the world anymore. Essentially, I was supposed to have a personal relationship with God as long as it fit into the box they had constructed for me, and I was supposed to allow the Holy Spirit to guide my life, but only in the direction they be-lieved the Holy Spirit led people.

During the deconstruction process, I came to terms with this dichotomy and tore it to the ground. I left the rubble for a bit before reconstructing it completely. It took me time to sort through all the debris and figure out what I believed about certain aspects of my relationship with God. For example, I struggled with what I believed about speaking in tongues and prophesying.

It wasn't that I doubted the presence of the Holy Spirit in my life or that I thought I had to speak in tongues or prophesy to prove I had the Holy Spirit living in me. But I still struggled with the belief that had been ingrained in my brain my entire life that these spiritual practices no longer existed. As I was attempting to reconstruct a faith that would allow me to breathe again and live in peace, I found that I kept wondering if it wasn't that I was closed off to these spiritual practices because of my upbringing but instead the fact that they no longer existed in our world.

During this time, I met some amazing, beautiful, faithful women of God from a different Christian tradition than my own, and they opened my eyes to what it looks like to truly be open to the leading of the Holy Spirit. God sent these women into my life in the middle of my Holy Spirit crisis as beacons of hope and healing and to show me that my personal relationship with God didn't have to fit in a box, be tied to a performance, or be conditional based on my behavior.

For the majority of my life, the only verse I was taught from I Corinthians 14 was verse 5, when Paul tells the Corinthians that if they speak in tongues, there should be an interpreter. Looking back now, it feels like they chose to ignore everything else Paul was saying throughout that chapter. These godly women God saw fit to intersect me with didn't ignore the rest of the chapter at all. They fully embraced it.

They talked at length about praying in the spirit with groans that go beyond words, and they recognized Paul's words in verse

15, where he said: "So here's what I've concluded. I will pray in the Spirit, but I will also pray with my mind engaged. I will sing rapturous praises in the Spirit, but I will also sing with my mind engaged."[24] I needed to step back and look at this chapter and this theology with fresh eyes. I needed to be able to see the big picture and hear other voices to begin to reconstruct my faith related to these topics.

I realized as I began to reconstruct the truth about my personal relationship with God that I was going to have to apply those same principles to every area of my faith that needed to be rebuilt. I had torn it all to the ground, and I knew exactly what I didn't believe, but I was simply looking at a giant pile of rubble, trying to figure out what was trash, what was still good, and what could be repurposed. The only way to do that for me was to open my mind to what God was leading me to and telling me both inside of the church and outside of those four walls. Around every corner, I found myself questioning what I believed and why I believed that.

Forming an authentic belief system separate from the corporate church and from what I had always been taught became my top priority in my reconstruction. Once I realized my personal relationship with God was not contingent on all those things the church spent years telling me it was, an entire world opened up that showed me it wasn't just my relationship with God that was mine to develop and understand, it was every aspect of my faith that had to become personal.

MY BIBLE BOYFRIEND

I was in the middle of a messy divorce at the same time as I was attempting to reconstruct my faith and develop an authentic relationship with God. I'd love to sit here and tell you I had a reve-

---

[24] I Corinthians 14:15 TPT

lation, that God stepped into my living room and spoke to me, or even that something stirred my desire to start my reconstruction in the Psalms. As I look back on this now, I can see how the power of the Holy Spirit was at work in this, but I still can't tell you what it was that made me open the First 5 App and choose the Psalms. I mean, seriously – the plan is so long they had to split it into two plans. Yet, that's the plan I chose.

During this topsy-turvy time in my life, I was fortunate enough to be surrounded by an amazing circle who let me ask my questions without judgment and tag along with their husbands and families all the time. When we were blackballed from my childhood church, it wasn't long before our dear friends and youth pastors, Jeff and Jody, met the same fate. Throughout the years of starting a new church, trying to do church differently, and the implosion of my life, they were consistently by my side. Even as I deconstructed aspects of my faith they had been an integral part of, they still stood by me without judgment.

Jody was also working through her deconstruction journey during this time, but I'm not sure she recognized it until later, so we agreed to dig into the Psalms together. I have to be completely honest with you here—I had never read the Psalms in their entirety. I had read portions of individual Psalms, some whole Psalms, and snippets from others.

I'm not going to tell you where to start when it comes to finding the right text to help you begin your reconstruction because we are all so different and so are our experiences. I can tell you this, though: if you have been taught to believe that you have to bow your head, close your eyes, and maintain a certain posture before God, the Psalms are an amazing prayer journal that will help you heal, open your eyes to what honesty and authenticity look like when it comes to your relationship with God, and remind you that God is for you and not against you.

Within the first week of my study of Psalms, my emotions were all over the place because, again, I felt like I had been lied to about prayer, posture, etc., my entire life. I also felt immeasurable freedom as I read David's intimate thoughts and prayers. He's a man who didn't pull punches, and I admired that about him. As I continued to read through his private thoughts and guttural cries to God, I was overwhelmed by what his writing revealed about who he was as a person. This combination of failures/successes, rights/wrongs, and good/bad resonated with me on every single level.

There are just as many layers to David's story as there are to his personality. From his father's disgust with him as a boy to his violence as an adult to his heart-wrenching belief that God was for him and not against him, David was undeniably human – just like me. He was a hot mess – just like me. He was flawed – just like me. And I loved him for it.

I loved the fact that David could spend the entire first half of a prayer begging God to destroy his enemies, then pivot to acknowledging God's power and majesty before ending with a claim on rest and peace. Shauna Niequest speaks about this in *Present over Perfect*. She tells how her friend Geri told her to picture a bottle of oil and vinegar salad dressing:

> The vinegar, probably red wine vinegar, rests on the top of the olive oil, softly red, flecked with oregano. The green-yellow oil is at the bottom of the bottle, rich and flavorful. Geri said that when you begin to pray, pour out the vinegar first–the acid, whatever's troubling you, whatever hurt you, whatever is harsh and jangling your nerves or spirit. You pour that out first...
>
> Then what you find underneath is the oil, glistening and thick...This is the grounding truth of life with God, that

we're connected, that we're not alone, that life is not all vinegar–puckery and acidic. It is also oil, luscious, thick, heavy with history and flavor.[25]

This is how David prayed: he poured out his heart, and with it, he poured out all the vinegar so he could get to the luscious, rich oil. That's what I knew I wanted as the basis of my relationship with God. I wanted to be able to verbally pour out all the vinegar and not feel guilty, or like a whiner, or like God would love me less. But I also wanted to be able to access the oil. I wanted to feel the richness of the oil in my life and, like David, remember the majesty of God and the miracles of His ways and workings in my life.

I fell in love with God at the same time as I fell in love with the writings of David, who I affectionately referred to as my Bible boyfriend. Until I got remarried. My husband didn't really want to share me with a Bible character.

TRUTH VS. TRADITION

My deconstruction taught me about the vast void that often exists between truth and tradition, but my study of Psalms and the character of David taught me the depth of how much truth lay far beyond the limitations of those traditions and how much reconstruction work existed in front of me. I spent so much time during deconstruction looking at tenets and tearing them to the ground because of the lies they contained, but I hadn't yet reconstructed them. There was so much work in the deconstruction that I didn't have the energy or brainpower left to reconstruct at that point. My study of the Psalms, though, sparked an unbridled energy and need to dig deep into some of the most damaging tenets of my former belief system.

[25] Niequest, Shauna, Present over Perfect. Center Point Pub, 2017.

Reading the Psalms taught me what prayer was in a way I had never been taught before. I realized that if I could learn so much about prayer from David's heartfelt songs, then there must be so much more in the pages of that archaic text I had missed, misread, or misinterpreted throughout my life as well. I started on my quest to learn everything I could and reconstruct my faith in an authentic and true way instead of one that was learned and rehearsed.

I still don't have it all figured out. I wish I did, but sometimes I feel like this is a never-ending process. Just when I think I have one thing mastered, I find more, read more, and learn more. I've grown accustomed to that, though, just like I've grown accustomed to admitting when I'm wrong, apologizing for what I used to believe and even teach, and accepting that the truth might change depending on the factors attached to it.

It wasn't until I separated myself from the faulty theology I was raised in that I was able to see the forest *and* the trees. The forest just kept becoming clearer the further I walked away from the past, and the more consistently I could see the big picture. One of the most glaring big pictures I sat with and admired for quite some time was what I learned from Jesus's interaction with women.

The faith traditions of my youth taught me many negative and damaging traditions about women, their voices, and their roles in life and the church. Jesus, though, taught me so much more truth through His example. I have many favorite stories of Jesus interacting with women. I'd love to tell you what I learned from a few of them when I read them *without* the lens of my church upbringing.

Mary: When Jesus Turned Water into Wine

I've heard the story of Jesus turning water into wine as his first public miracle more times than I can count. Growing up, the story always focused on the miracle itself: the wedding ran out of wine, so Jesus turned water into wine. That's the end. Moving on.

I missed so much when I looked at this story through this lens. The details of this story are what make it such a testament to Christ and His relationship with people. Here's how John describes the scene in chapter 2 verses 1-10[26]:

> "Now on the third day, Jesus' mother went to a wedding feast in the Galilean village of Cana. Jesus and his disciples were all invited to the banquet, but with so many guests, they ran out of wine. And when Mary realized it, she came to Jesus and asked, "They have no wine; *can't you do something about it?*"

> Jesus replied, "My dear one, don't you understand that if I do this, it will change nothing for you, but it will change everything for me! My hour *of unveiling my power* has not yet come."

> Mary then went to the servers and told them, "Whatever Jesus tells you, do it!"

> Nearby stood six stone water pots meant to be used for the Jewish washing rituals. Each one could hold about twenty gallons or more. Jesus came to the servers and instructed them, "Fill the *pots with water, right up to the very brim.*" Then he said, "Now fill your pitchers and take them to the master of ceremonies."

> And when they poured out their pitchers for the master of ceremonies to sample, the water had become wine! When he tasted the water that had become wine, the master of ceremonies was impressed with its quality. (Although he didn't know where the wine had come from, only the servers knew.) He called the bridegroom over and said to

---

[26] John 2:1-10 TPT

him, "Every host serves his best wine first, until everyone has had a cup or two, then he serves the cheaper wine. But you, my friend, you've reserved the most exquisite wine until now!"

It was Mary, Jesus's mom, who came to Him and asked Him to do something. His *mom*.

I can picture the scene, can't you? The wedding celebration is in full swing, and soon, people start to realize the wine has run out. I don't know about you, but I've never been to a wedding where the wine ran out; however, I can imagine how that might put a damper on the festivities.

I can see Jesus reclining with His buddies when Mary approaches with those puppy-dog eyes, asking for Jesus, her son, to save the day and the wedding feast. There are so many ways Jesus could have responded to His mom. He could have simply told her no. He could have told her He wasn't wasting a miracle on something so trivial. He could have told her it wasn't worth outing himself as the Messiah just so people could have some wine at a wedding. He could have said so many things.

Instead, He looks at this woman – His mom, who was probably in her mid-forties – and asks her if she understands what she is asking of Him. He explains to her that nothing will change for her, but everything will change for him because it wasn't yet time for Him to reveal His identity.

But He does it anyway.

His mother, a woman, asks Him to save the day for their friends and family at this wedding, and He does it for her, them, His friends, and His family.

I don't know about you, but this isn't the way I was ever taught this story. This isn't the Jesus I was introduced to. This loving, compassionate, understanding man who gave a woman His full attention is not the same as the strict, unbending, distant Jesus I was raised with. And I like this guy so much better.

Jesus and the Woman at the Well

This is another one of those stories I heard so many times throughout my childhood that I had it memorized. Or, I had memorized what I was told to memorize and ignored the rest of the details of the story. The end of this story struck me when I read it without the lens I had been raised with. You can find the full account of the Samaritan woman at the well in John 4. In this chapter, John explains how she was at the well in the middle of the day, that Jesus went and sat down beside her, how they talk some Jewish history, and how Jesus offered her living water right before He revealed to her that He knows she's been married five times and that the man she lives with isn't her husband.

Those details were always the focus of this story when it was taught throughout my church upbringing. It's what happens next, though, that is the most important aspect of this story in my mind. In verses 27-30, John says:

> At that moment, his disciples returned and were stunned to see Jesus speaking with a Samaritan woman, yet none of them dared ask him why or what they were discussing. All at once, the woman left her water jar and ran off to her village and told everyone, "Come and meet a man at the well who told me everything I've ever done! He could be the One we've been waiting for." Hearing this, the people came streaming out of the village to go see Jesus.[27]

And then, in verses 39-41, John tells us:

> Many from the Samaritan village became believers in Jesus because of the woman's testimony: "He told me everything

---

[27] John 4:27-30 TPT

I ever did!" Then they begged Jesus to stay with them, so he stayed there for two days, resulting in many more coming to faith in him because of his message.[28]

Here's this woman who is thought to be an outcast in her Samaritan village getting her water in the middle of the day to avoid people, and when she encounters Jesus, she leaves everything behind to go tell the village – the very people she was avoiding - about Him. A little research will reveal that this Samaritan, though unnamed in scripture, is thought to be a woman named Photini[29]. She was named a disciple of Christ and eventually martyred because of it. She was one of the first evangelists of the New Testament, and many people came to know Christ because of her.

For years and years, I was taught that women couldn't minister or teach men. I was taught that women were inferior spiritually, and really in every way, to men. But... this. This woman sits with Jesus and is so changed by a single conversation with Him that she leaves everything and tells everyone – not just women and children. She becomes a mouthpiece for Christ, and she is eventually killed for it.

Do you know what I don't see happening in this interaction with Christ? I don't see Him looking at this woman and telling her how glad He is that her life has changed, but that she should probably only go and tell the other women and the children in the village about him because she is a woman. I don't see Jesus limiting her reach or silencing her voice based on her lifestyle or her gender. So much of my upbringing in my childhood church revolved around gender roles and who women could teach. Here, though, Jesus doesn't focus on gender at all.

---

[28] John 4:39-41 TPT

[29] "Martyr Photini the Samaritan Woman, Her Sons, and Those with Them." Orthodox Church in America, 20 Mar. 2024, www.oca.org/saints/lives/2013/03/20/100846-martyr-photini-the-samaritan-woman-her-sons-and-those-with-them.

Instead, I see Jesus sitting down with a woman who was oppressed due to her religious beliefs, marginalized because of her gender, and an outcast because of her relationships and empowering her to become a powerful disciple in his ministry.

That's the Jesus I want to know.

THE QUEST FOR TRUTH

The more I studied stories I thought I knew inside and out, the more I realized I barely knew them at all. The Jesus I thought I knew was nowhere close to the Jesus in these stories, and that's the Jesus I wanted to know and the Jesus whose ways I wanted to mirror. That quickly became the focus of my reconstruction journey – to know Jesus, who He was, what He did, and how He treated people.

On this reconstruction journey, your priorities might look different than mine. The aspects of your faith that you are attempting to rebuild very well might be completely different from mine. And do you know what? That's completely okay. If you're like me, you've spent your life with people telling you what boxes to tick, what rules to follow, and what stickers you get for your "good Christian" sticker chart. But that isn't the way it has to be.

Your faith has to be your own.

As you work through this reconstruction journey, let me encourage you to sit with that for as long as you need - to understand your priorities for reconstruction and determine where you need to start and what you need to focus on. Then, tackle what's most important to you first. If your top priority is to raise kids who can think critically and who aren't bound by the rules and regulations of fundamentalism, then start there. If your priority is to determine what Jesus thought about gender, then start there. If your priority is to figure out what Jesus said about communion, start there. And, if your priority is something totally different, then start there. Your journey is your own, and your priorities are yours alone.

It doesn't matter what anyone else is doing on their reconstruction journey. We are all individuals, and our experiences are unique. You might even find that you and your siblings experienced the same things, but your response to them and your priorities in reconstruction look completely different. And you know what? That's okay. Trauma looks different for everyone.

I would suggest creating a plan of attack for those things you are struggling with and don't have answers for. For me, that meant starting in the Psalms and learning how to be authentic with God. That was just the beginning, though. That foundation gave me what I needed to approach God and ask him to guide the course of my journey, which allowed me the confidence I needed in my quest for truth.

What I found in my own studies was that there are so many tools right at my fingertips. I could open an app and have access to dozens of translations. I could easily access the context of Scripture, have the original Greek and Hebrew in front of me in the blink of an eye, and read endless scholars in minutes. I didn't have to rely on faulty theology thrown at me from the pulpit or uneducated Sunday School teachers because I had access to more research and information than I ever even knew existed. And you do, too.

There are many scholars and experts out there who are doing the hard work, too. Their research is invaluable. When you identify what topics you want to dig deeply into, find the experts on those topics and read their work. Read it all so you can come to conclusions you own for yourself.

My journey didn't just stop with my own research, though. I quickly realized there were entire communities out there who were struggling with the same questions I had and who were seeking their own truths, just like I was. I became a part of those communities. I followed those people and organizations on social media. I read their books and their blog posts, and I found camaraderie and companionship through what has the potential to be a terribly lonely process. You can do that too. You can find this companionship and these communities as well.

Finally, as you embark on this long and arduous journey, let me encourage you to take breaks when your mind, body, and soul are telling you to take breaks. This is mentally, emotionally, and spiritually exhausting work. When your soul is telling you to step away for a minute, listen intently to it, and step away. Burnout doesn't look good on any of us, and most of us have lived through so much spiritual burnout in our lives, we owe ourselves a break. You owe yourself a break, friend.

REFLECTIONS: WHAT MATTERS MOST

Remember:

- You never have to be "fine."
- You don't have to have all the answers or even any of the answers.
- Nothing can separate you from the love of God–not even your deconstruction and reconstruction.
- Our relationships with God need to be our personal relationships and not based on corporate relationships.
- David and his psalms are an authentic example of prayer.
- We have to pour out the vinegar to get to the oil.
- Truth is different than tradition.
- Start with your top priorities.
- Utilize your resources, connections, communities, and experts.
- Take a break.

Receive:
Romans 8:38-39 TPT:

So now I live with the confidence that there is nothing in the universe with the power to separate us from God's love. I'm convinced that his love will triumph over death, life's troubles, fallen angels, or dark rulers in the heavens. There is nothing in our present or future circumstances that can weaken his love. There is no power above us or beneath us—no power that could ever be found in the universe that can distance us from God's passionate love, which is lavished upon us through our Lord Jesus, the Anointed One!

Lamentations 3: 22-23 MSG:

God's loyal love couldn't have run out,
    his merciful love couldn't have dried up.
They're created new every morning.
    How great your faithfulness!

I'm sticking with God (I say it over and over).

He's all I've got left.

I John 1: 8-9 TPT:

If we boast that we have no sin, we're only fooling ourselves and are strangers to the truth. But if we freely admit our sins *when his light uncovers them*, he will be faithful to forgive us every time. God is just to forgive us our sins *because of Christ*, and he will continue to cleanse us from all unrighteousness. (emphasis added)

Philippians 1:3-6 TPT:

My prayers for you are full of praise to God as I give him thanks for you with great joy! I'm so grateful for our union and our enduring partnership that began the first time I presented to you the gospel. I pray with great faith for you, because I'm fully convinced that the One who began this gracious work in you will faithfully continue the process of maturing you until the unveiling of our Lord Jesus Christ!

Reflect:

1. Brainstorm the habits, emotions, and spiritual practices you have as a result of faulty theology, church hurt, or religious trauma. What are the detrimental things you need to leave behind?
2. Read through some of David's psalms and think about how he pours out the vinegar to get to the rich oil in his prayer life.
3. Spend this week working on how you can reconstruct your relationship with God in an authentic way where you can comfortably pour out all the vinegar first and then sit with the good, rich oil.
4. What are your top priorities as you move forward on your reconstruction journey?
5. Get online and find your community. Don't do this alone.

Prayer:

God, this is hard work. Changing my habits and abandoning the spiritual beliefs and faith practices of my past is hard. I'm not always good at it. I'm going to make mistakes. I'm going to get frustrated. I'm tired already. But, God, I know that there is nothing I can do that will separate me from your love. I know that it doesn't matter how well I perform or how well I fit into a box that determines how much you love me or care about me. I know that you are good and that you have promised you will give me new mercies every morning. God, remind me of those things every day as I face this long and exhausting journey of reconstruction ahead of me.

VII

LAYING YOUR FAITH FOUNDATION:
IDENTIFYING YOUR NON-NEGOTIABLES

Christmas break of 1993 had finally arrived, and I was excited to relax, hang out with my friends and family, spend time with my boyfriend, and catch up on the past issue of my favorite magazine for teen Christian girls. Flopping down on my bed, I opened the magazine and was immediately drawn to an article discussing healthy dating habits for Christian teens.

Convinced this article was going to confirm that I was doing everything correctly in my relationship with my boyfriend, I started reading. Immediately, I started to feel sick to my stomach. The author of the article discussed how Christians should not waste their time dating guys they didn't want to marry. I panicked. Did I want to marry my boyfriend? Was he the man God had picked out for me?

I couldn't answer either of those questions with an unwavering yes, so I knew what I had to do. Several days passed where I didn't see my boyfriend. The night he showed up with my Christmas gift and a smile, I broke up with him and broke his heart. After all, that was God's will, right?

This terrible magazine article spurred me to break up with a perfectly nice and respectable boyfriend at 14 because that article insisted that God did not want me to date anyone I wouldn't marry. As a naive and idealistic 14-year-old, I was not convinced I would want to marry this poor, sweet soul, so I did what every God-fearing and Christian magazine-reading 14-year-old would do: I broke up with him and broke his heart for absolutely no good reason. Just to be clear here – no, I didn't have any idea what marriage should be, what I should be looking for in a spouse, or any clear picture of marriage. Because I was 14. And somehow, I thought God was going to magically reveal to me who and what I needed in marriage by only dating people I thought I could marry.

It makes sense, right? Only date people who you could marry, even though you have no idea who you are compatible with, what you might need in a relationship, what works for you, what is best for you, etc. And again, I find myself needing to bang my head against the wall because, no. This is absurd and makes no logical or relational sense. And yet, at 14, I believed this was my path to a healthy and happy marriage where we would live happily ever after.

Just a few years later, I found myself at a Christian college where sayings like "ring in spring" and "M.R.S. degrees" weren't merely lip service but reality. As a spiritually, mentally, and emotionally healthy adult, looking back on these years of my life makes me a little nauseous and also makes me want to bang my head against a wall because not much has changed on the Christian College scene. It's honestly all so cringy that I'm a bit ashamed I was part of it.

Even though no one came right out and said that it was everyone's goal to find the perfect Christian spouse at said Christian College, that was the goal. The majority of us were raised in purity culture and were victims of the terrible advice and theology that came through those teen bibles of the 80s and 90s and the ever-popular Christian magazines. I was no exception. I got engaged at 19, after just a few short months of dating.

I would love to be able to tell you that my beliefs and behaviors changed as I matured and went to college, but that would be a complete lie. They didn't change at all. If anything, I think they just expanded and got worse. Then, it took me until I was 38 years old to begin to disentangle myself from those beliefs and behaviors. For me, part of that was divorce.

Everyone deals with divorce differently, just like everyone deals with deconstruction and reconstruction differently. I chose a path of growth, healing, and peace. I was determined to never repeat the same mistakes I made in my first marriage, so I went to therapy. I talked. I listened. I was validated. I grew. I healed. For the first time in my life, I was choosing health over harm and function over dysfunction, and I was bound and determined I was going to apply those tactics to every aspect of my life. I would never again allow myself to be at rock bottom, to be at such a place where I would make terrible decisions that would implode my life, and would never again allow another person to make me feel the way I had felt for all those years.

I emerged from therapy, from that season, and from divorce, an entirely different version of me. I don't want to say I was a completely different person because I'm still the same person, but I'm an authentic version of myself now instead of a hollow version I allowed other people to fill as I did in my first marriage.

When you've been married for decades, and you find yourself in the middle of a divorce, it's easy to feel like no one will ever love you again. Often, I think that is one of the key reasons why people stay in terrible marriages: they choose the dysfunction they know and are comfortable with instead of facing the unknown and risking never being loved again. One of the things God whispered to me over and over again through that time was that I was worthy of love and my needs were important.

I took this seriously. I heard God's voice, and I heeded his nudges. I had this beautiful leather-bound journal where I poured out my heart throughout that terrible period. I began to listen to my soul, my body, my mind, and my emotions, and on the last five pages of it, I began a list of what I needed in a relationship and a partner. Whenever I discovered something new or had a revelation about one of my needs, I wrote it down in the back of that journal. Then, when more details would come to me, I'd flip to the back of the journal and expand on the ideas that I had.

That list became my non-negotiables for my relationships. If I was in a situation where I thought about dating someone, I would flip to that list as a reminder of what God and I had decided were my non-negotiables. It was four years before I met someone who didn't force me to compromise on any of my non-negotiables on that list. I knew within a week of meeting Russ that he was getting dangerously close to ticking off all the boxes on my non-negotiable list, and eventually, I copied the list for him into his own journal so he would know exactly how God had prepared my heart for him for four years.

If I hadn't taken the time to go through therapy, to heal, to find peace with myself, and to listen as God helped me identify my non-negotiables for my relationships, I would have floated around like a ship lost at sea. My non-negotiables became the anchor for my romantic relationships. The same is true for my faith, though. Throughout the deconstruction process, I was left with so much rubble to sort through and a skeleton to reconstruct from. In the same way I had to identify my non-negotiables for my romantic life, I had to determine my non-negotiables for my faith life. I needed to know what my foundation was for reconstructing my faith, but I couldn't do that until I took the time to figure out what was not negotiable for me in terms of faith, religion, God, Jesus, and people. Once I identified those non-negotiables, I had something to reconstruct from that I knew wasn't going to collapse on or around me.

I'm going to spend the next few pages discussing my non-negotiables and how I arrived at them, and I pray that during this time, God will help you identify those things that will become your non-negotiables as well.

1. JESUS IS LOVE IN ACTION

I'm going to be completely transparent with you here: I don't have all the answers. I don't know which stories in the Bible are meant to be taken literally and which are metaphors. I don't know why God chose to do some of the things that He did in the Old Testament. I don't know. I wish I knew - kind of. But, part of me is okay with not knowing, with accepting that there are forces out there that are infinitely bigger than me and that know infinitely more than me. If this is your struggle, let me encourage you to check out some amazing scholars who have written at length on these topics. You can't go wrong with Heather Hamilton's *Returning to Eden* or Rachel Held Evans's *Inspired*, and if you want to dig into an intellectual discussion of myth, Joseph Campbell's *The Power of Myth*. I am not an expert, and I would leave you with more questions than answers on that front. For me, that wasn't one of my non-negotiables.

Here's what I do know and what is one of my non-negotiables: Jesus is love in action. I appreciate Luke. I admire his attention to detail. I'm impressed by the way he recorded his interpretation of how Jesus was love in action throughout His life. While I can't wrap my head around some of the decisions God made in the Old Testament, I can say with 100% assuredness that Jesus came to be love in action, and that is the model I am going to follow.

Reading Luke's account on my own without the lens of my church upbringing showed me many details about Jesus's life and love that I had missed for years. I'm confident I would have continued to miss them if I hadn't made the conscious choice to read Luke through a different lens. If you're struggling with where to start on this reconstruction journey and understanding who Jesus was as a human when He walked the earth, I would turn you to the book of Luke.

The lens of Jesus is the lens through which everything passes for me – not Paul's lens, even though he wrote an absurd amount of what the council of Nicaea chose as our Bible–and not the Old Testament God lens. While I can acknowledge that there are definitely some good nuggets in Paul's books, and while I know those letters served an amazing purpose in their context and for their intended audience, if we only read Paul's letters and ignore the example and teachings of Jesus, we are surely missing the point. There are so many things that are "Biblical" according to Paul's letters, but that aren't Jesus-like in the least bit. When we take those directives meant for a specific church in an archaic time and we attempt to translate them, or simply transfer them to today and our churches, we run a major risk of taking Jesus out of the equation all together. If we aren't careful, we can make our faith and faith communities about a man (Paul) instead of about The Messiah. That's an important distinction.

2. PEOPLE ARE FLAWED–NOT BROKEN

When you think of broken, what's the first thing that comes to mind? For me, I immediately think of something that needs to be fixed or mended first and then something that is broken beyond repair. As a parent, this one really hits home. I can't imagine looking at Kate and telling her she's broken, or worse, telling her that God created her as broken so that He could fix her. No way. As her mom, what I would be much more likely to tell her is the overwhelming message of Psalm 139:[30]

> "Lord, you know everything there is to know about me.
>
> You perceive every movement of my heart and soul,
> and you understand my every thought before it even enters my mind.
>
> You are so intimately aware of me, Lord.
> You read my heart like an open book
> and you know all the words I'm about to speak
>
> before I even start a sentence!
> You know every step I will take before my journey even begins.
>
> You've gone into my future to prepare the way,
> and in kindness you follow behind me
> to spare me from the harm of my past.
> You have laid your hand on me!
>
> This is just too wonderful, deep, and incomprehensible!
> Your understanding of me brings me wonder and strength.
>
> Where could I go from your Spirit?
> Where could I run and hide from your face?
>
> If I go up to heaven, you're there!
> If I go down to the realm of the dead, you're there too!
>
> If I fly with wings into the shining dawn, you're there!
> If I fly into the radiant sunset, you're there waiting!

---

[30] Psalm 139 TPT

Wherever I go, your hand will guide me;
your strength will empower me.

It's impossible to disappear from you
or to ask the darkness to hide me,
for your presence is everywhere, bringing light into my night.

There is no such thing as darkness with you.
The night, to you, is as bright as the day;
there's no difference between the two.

You formed my innermost being, shaping my delicate inside
and my intricate outside,
and wove them all together in my mother's womb.

I thank you, God, for making me so mysteriously complex!
Everything you do is marvelously breathtaking.
It simply amazes me to think about it!
How thoroughly you know me, Lord!

You even formed every bone in my body
when you created me in the secret place;
carefully, skillfully you shaped me from nothing to something.

You saw who you created me to be before I became me!
Before I'd ever seen the light of day,
the number of days you planned for me
were already recorded in your book.

Every single moment you are thinking of me!
How precious and wonderful to consider
that you cherish me constantly in your every thought!
O God, your desires toward me are more
than the grains of sand on every shore!
When I awake each morning, you're still with me."

This is the heart of David. We've already talked about how he's an extremely flawed man with his fair share of weakness. Those flaws and weaknesses didn't make him broken, though, and our flaws and weaknesses don't make us broken, either. They make us imperfect people, and that is an important distinction. As far as I can tell, the idea that we are all broken people originated from the ideas of people broken into pieces like pieces of pottery in Isaiah, as well as Paul explaining how Christ is made perfect in Paul's weakness.[31] These are both such a stretch, though, and they are dangerous theology.

This is one of my key non-negotiables, but it is also one that has taken me the longest to arrive at and accept. I spent my entire life in the church hearing that we are all broken people. I still hear it in my church today, and I love my church – except for this part. When Jesus first stood up in the synagogue in His hometown of Nazareth after his ministry started, He quoted Isaiah, saying this:

> "The Spirit of the Lord is upon me, and he has anointed me to be hope for the poor, healing for the brokenhearted, and new eyes for the blind, and to preach to prisoners, 'You are set free!' I have come to share the message of Jubilee, for the time of God's great acceptance has begun."[32]

I don't see anywhere here where Jesus says He has come to heal the broken. What He does say, though, is that He has come to be hope for the poor, healing for the *brokenhearted*, new eyes for the blind, and freedom for the prisoners. That's a distinction we can't ignore, friends. Being *broken* and being *brokenhearted* are two very different things.

Jesus came to be hope, healing, and freedom. Because we're each imperfect and have individual weaknesses, we need the hope,

---

[31] Isaiah 30:14-16

[32] Luke 4:18-19 TPT

healing, and freedom we find in Him, and we need to offer those things to others. We need to stop looking at ourselves and each other as if we are broken, and especially as if we are broken beyond repair.

3. GOD CREATED ME IN HIS IMAGE, BUT HE GAVE ME MY OWN IDENTITY

There was this massive paradox that existed in the theology of my church upbringing that preached that I was fearfully and wonderfully made in God's image, but my identity was completely dependent on how well I ticked off boxes, followed rules, performed, was moral, and practiced selflessness. Consequently, my identity was always in question because it was tied to my actions and not to who God actually created me to be.

On one hand, I was taught that God created me to be wonderful in His own image. On the other hand, though, I had to work every day to achieve that image or to be worthy of it. For the record, this is a completely impossible task. When we're raised to believe that our identity is inextricably tied to our behavior and our actions, that results in all sorts of unhealthy behaviors like perfectionism, people-pleasing, and self-loathing.

It also creates an unbreakable bond between our jobs, relationships, church service, successes/failures, and our identity, which results in our inability to separate our identities from those things in our lives. We become defined by our:

- Jobs
- Relationships
- Volunteerism
- Service

Disentangling my identity from those external factors and my actions was a challenge. I spent so many years attributing who I was to what I was doing and achieving that I struggled to figure out who God created me to be apart from those things. For me to kill my insatiable desire to achieve, I had to sever the thread that tied my achievements to my identity and accept that God created me as a human – not as a robot designed solely for success and achievement.

I tried to figure out where this faulty theology comes from, and I think it's from a combination of the concept behind the fruit we bear and Paul's discussion in Galatians, where he says that he no longer lives, but Christ lives in him.[33] Combine that with the constant warnings throughout Scripture related to being haughty, proud, and arrogant, and voila – we subconsciously feel like we have to achieve and perform in a way that isn't too proud but still displays all the good fruit we're producing.

That's exhausting, isn't it? And it completely misses the point. We shouldn't bear good fruit to prove how good we are, how close to God we are, or how successful of a Christian we are. No, our closeness to God and our desire to be like Christ will inevitably result in our good fruit as Christ is alive in us. We have to shift that narrative and recognize it isn't our fruit that marks us as "Christ-like" as much as it is our desire to be like Christ that results in our good fruit.

I endeavor to live my life knowing that I have been fearfully and wonderfully made in the image of God and that God gifted me with this unique identity that is not dependent on what I'm doing, what job I have, how many hours of service I perform, or what ministries I volunteer for at my church. Instead of focusing on the fruit I'm bearing, I focus on my relationship with my Creator, knowing the fruit will come as a natural consequence of that relationship.

---

[33] Galatians 2:20

And friend, that is what freedom looks like in my life. That's what allows me to breathe deeply without the pressure of performance or achievement. My God loves me just the way I am because He made me this way on purpose and with purpose. As I've said before, and I'll probably say again another ten times, there is nothing I can do that will separate me from His unconditional love, but also, there's nothing I can do that can make His unconditional love any greater either. He's not going to love me more because of my successes, just like He won't love me less because of my failures. True freedom, friends.

4. GRACE ISN'T STATIC

I fell in love with grace so much as an adult that it became the subject of my first tattoo. I spent so many years in a church that never mentioned grace that once I began to understand grace, I never wanted to be without it again. One of the most terrifying and traumatizing experiences I ever had in church happened when I was in a 5th-grade Sunday School class. This Sunday School teacher, we'll call him Steve, told us, as 11 and 12-year-olds, that when we die, all of our sins were going to be played like a movie for everyone to see, and we would have to explain all of our poor choices while everyone watched the movie of our sins play and listened to our explanation. Even writing that gives me the heebie-jeebies.

As an intelligent and healed adult who loves God, my initial response to that is, "Are you freaking kidding me right now?" And at the thought of this being taught to kids as a parent myself, my secondary response is, "Would you care to discuss this outside?" Because, seriously? No. Where is the grace in this? The forgiveness? The casting my sins into the depths of forgetfulness?

I'll tell you where it is – non-existent. And sadly, that's the fear I lived my life in for over 30 years. Even as I read my Bible and other texts and grew in my knowledge of and relationship with God, I still feared the God who would do this.

I am forever grateful for the gifts of deconstruction and reconstruction that taught me how flawed the idea is of my sins being shown as a movie for everyone to see. I'm grateful for deconstruction and reconstruction showing me how the Jesus who walked this earth and the God who loved me as a father are both grace and love incarnate. And grace and love incarnate are not about to project my sins onto a movie screen while we all sit around and watch them. Grace and love have already forgotten about each one of those sins in favor of a running embrace and a party.

And then another running embrace and another party.

And another.

And another.

Because grace and love are not static. There are no finite amounts of each of them. I cannot exhaust my share of them. It's not about me getting my fair share of either or ever getting what I deserve. Grace is unfair that way; there's always more to go around.

5. HOPE FOR TODAY

Have you ever been around people who view their lives on earth as a test and a curse? They live their lives on earth for the sole purpose of the afterlife. They frequently say things like, "This world is not my home," and they talk about how they're simply biding their time until they can get to heaven. I spent years surrounded by people who unashamedly held those attitudes, and it is seriously depressing and sucks the life right out of you.

This is one of those ideologies that doesn't make a lick of sense when you take a step back from it and look at it. Do you think God created humanity so they would have to suffer through 100 or so years here on earth longing for their heavenly home? Why? Why would anyone do that?

We frequently take archaic concepts and attempt to translate them into our world today, and this is one of those concepts that has been pulled this way, bent that way, and manipulated another way to arrive at this conclusion. The reason this has happened is likely because of a fear of hell so many people and churches carry around with them. Jesus didn't focus on hell, though. He literally preached that the kingdom of heaven is now.[34] We aren't supposed to be simply holding our breath and waiting to die so we can experience the kingdom of heaven; we're supposed to be living like we're in the kingdom of heaven now, and we can't do that without hope for the world today.

That's why this is one of my non-negotiables. I refuse to live my life for tomorrow alone when God has given me endless hope for today. Even when the world around me seems daunting, hopeless, and like all is lost, I will never have victory and fulfillment if I can't cling to the hope that God has given me today and the knowledge that I am living in the kingdom of heaven right now.

6. LOVE GOD. LOVE PEOPLE.

If you've never sat down and read John's account of the Last Supper in chapter 13, I would encourage you to stop and do that right now. The example Jesus sets for us on his last night with His best friends is amazing, and I can't help but think if more people were like this Jesus, the world would be a completely different place.

First, at the beginning of the chapter, John explains how Jesus took the place of a servant and washed the feet of His disciples. One concept I've been clinging to in this season of my life is that it is really difficult to throw stones and wash people's feet at the same

---

[34] Luke 17:20

time. It's pretty close to impossible. Yet, we live in a world and attend churches where throwing stones is much more common than washing feet.

My favorite part of this story happens after the foot-washing, the meal, the analogy that would become communion, and the betrayal. It comes in verses 34 and 35 when John explains that Jesus told them:

> "So I give you now a new commandment: Love each other just as much as I have loved you. For when you demonstrate the same love I have for you by loving one another, everyone will know that you're my true followers."[35]

I'm pretty confident the mic drop didn't exist in Christ's day, but if it did, this seems like this would have been the ideal place for it. We make this so much more difficult than it needs to be. Our goal is love – loving God and loving people like Christ loved and served them. This wasn't negotiable for Christ, and it is not negotiable for me either.

I take this seriously when it comes to the faith communities with which I align myself. Love has to be the basis of the faith community, or I know it isn't for me. The same is true in my relationships. If dogma, theology, and rules are the driving forces in a person's life, I keep an emotional, mental, and spiritual distance. I know the damage that theology can do when it is placed above people and above love, and I know I can't be close to it ever again.

7. REDEMPTION AND RESTORATION

For so long, I only read the Bible through the lens of my childhood church. Everything changed for me when I started reading the Bible through the lens of literary analysis. I started to read Bible Sto-

---

[35] John 13:34-35 TPT

ries differently. If you've been in the church for any length of time, and especially if you grew up in a church going to Sunday School as a kid, you probably know most of the famous Bible Stories, and you could probably even recite most of them to me right now.

There are so many details in those famous Bible stories I missed for decades, and they point to the same thing–God is a God of redemption and restoration because most of the people He called and used were seriously messed up and flawed human beings. When we ignore those details of the lives of our Bible heroes and only focus on their heroic deeds, I fear that we miss the entire point. Here are some of my favorites:

- Adam and Eve walked in the Garden of Eden with God daily, and they still ate the fruit.[36]
- David was anointed a king, defeated Goliath, led Israel, and was a man after God's own heart, but he was also an adulterer/rapist (depending on which scholar you read), a conspirator, a murderer, and a man hellbent on vengeance. Yet, he is still revered and considered to be a man after God's own heart.[37]
- Tamar was mistreated terribly by her father-in-law, who she then seduced, disguised as a prostitute, getting pregnant in the process, and ending up in the lineage of Jesus.[38]
- Judah, Tamar's father-in-law, had sex with who he thought was a prostitute, but he still went on to be the ancestor of one of the twelve tribes of Israel.
- Jacob, Judah's dad, stole his brother's birthright, married sisters, and manipulated his father-in-law, but he was still renamed Israel, and his sons/grandsons were the patriarchs of the twelve tribes of Israel.[39]

---

[36] Genesis 3

[37] I Samuel

[38] Genesis 38

[39] Genesis 27

- Rahab was a prostitute, yet she found her way into Jesus's lineage.[40]
- Noah built the ark, but he also had a bit of an alcohol problem.[41]
- Moses murdered a man, but God still chose him to lead his people out of Egypt.[42]
- Sarah gave her maid to her husband because she wasn't getting pregnant, but God still chose her as the matriarch of Israel.[43]

Do I need to go on?

I struggle with how we can read these incredible stories of these very human individuals whom God chose over and over again, who He redeemed and restored over and over again, and yet, we still struggle with seeing how God can use us, or maybe how He can use them, or how He can use those people. There are no asterisks in God's stories that disqualify anyone from redemption and restoration and that keep them from being another miraculous bullet point on that list. That's not negotiable for me.

8. CHURCH PEOPLE AREN'T ALWAYS "GOOD" PEOPLE

This might be controversial, but if you've made it this far, I'm assuming you understand this all too well. Not all churches are created equally, and church people aren't always the "good" people. Sometimes, churches can be the most damaging, toxic, and traumatic institutions, and sometimes, the people in them can be the furthest thing from the Jesus who walked this earth.

---

[40] Joshua 2

[41] Genesis 9

[42] Exodus 2

[43] Genesis 26

This is a tough one. Because love and grace. God and Jesus are love and grace incarnate, and my goal is to follow the example of Christ. Not everyone will agree with this one, but sometimes, I have to love people from a distance because of boundaries. I'd be lying to you if I said there wasn't a constant battle waging in my soul between calling out the churches that are damaging so many people and attempting to love the people in those churches like Jesus. I lose that battle often.

Here's what I know to be true: all humans are flawed, and we inevitably screw up anything we touch. Sadly, the church is no different. While God is the theoretical head of the church, the reality is that it is still run by man, and it is undoubtedly going to be flawed. Every single church will have flaws because every single person has flaws. I have to discern what flaws I can live with, just like I have to choose what flaws are deal-breakers for me.

While this might seem like a strange non-negotiable, it's become one of my guiding principles to remember that people are flawed and that churches are no different. It keeps me vigilant but also allows me to show a little more grace than I want to at times.

IDENTIFYING YOUR NON-NEGOTIABLES:

It's taken me quite a few years to identify my non-negotiables, but I know that it's an important part of this reconstruction journey. Some of you can probably sit down and make a list of your non-negotiables right now. You know what aspects of your thinking you won't ever compromise again because you have worked hard to heal from that thinking. If you're one of those people, I would encourage you to take a break, step away, and make that list right now.

Others might not be as confident in their list of non-negotiables. You might have some ideas about the things you know you don't want to compromise on ever again and the driving principles of your life, but you've never taken the time to sit down and process them completely.

If you're in this category, I encourage you to sit down with a blank piece of paper right now or with a blank document/note on your device and spend 3-5 minutes freewriting about this. You might be surprised by what your subconscious wants to bring to the surface based on your past, your deconstruction, and your progress on this reconstruction journey.

Once you've completed your freewriting, go grab a few highlighters and look for themes in your freewriting. What are the ideas you come back to time and time again? What are the different ideas you can't seem to shake now, even as you've finished brainstorming? And if you need more time to freewrite, go back and keep writing until you get all your thoughts down on paper. Then, go through and look for themes. You might be surprised at the thoughts that pop up over and over again.

Once you have those themes, you can identify what about these themes makes them non-negotiables for you. Or, maybe you need to do a little research to see exactly where you stand or what you think about some of your themes.

Finally, become an expert on those non-negotiables. Don't just stop with identifying them, but dig into them. Find out what scholars are saying, read articles by the experts, join Facebook groups about the topics, and immerse yourself in learning everything you can about these topics because there is a reason they are on your list of non-negotiables.

Be diligent in your research. Lots of people have opinions, and not every opinion you find in a Facebook group, blog post, or Substack will be well-researched. Consider the source of what you're reading and be willing to walk away from information and opinions that don't serve you and your process well.

WORTHY WORK

When I finally had my list of non-negotiables, I began to feel like I was getting somewhere. I felt like my wounds had become scars, and I could make real progress on my reconstruction journey. While this is hard work, it's also the worthy work of healing and moving your life forward as a survivor. You deserve that. You deserve to know you are an overcomer and a survivor, and you deserve to know and own what's important to you on this faith journey.

REFLECTIONS: LAYING YOUR FAITH FOUNDATION

Remember:

- Your faith foundation is still intact even though you've deconstructed it.

- You have to sort through the rubble of your deconstruction if you want to reconstruct.

- Your non-negotiables are yours and yours alone; no one else has to understand them.

- Identifying your non-negotiables can take time.

Receive:

John 13:34-35 TPT

"So I give you now a new commandment: Love each other just as much as I have loved you. For when you demonstrate the same love I have for you by loving one another, everyone will know that you're my true followers."

Reflect:

1. Free-writing exercise: Take 3-5 minutes and write about your non-negotiables.
2. Organize your thoughts based on your free writing.
3. Pull out the themes/ideas that kept coming up.
4. Elaborate on why these are non-negotiables for you.
5. Become an expert
    a. Read
    b. Research
    c. Find the experts already

Prayer:

God, thank you for reminding me that I still have a firm faith foundation despite this hard work of deconstruction and reconstruction. Help me identify the non-negotiables of that faith foundation and understand them and the role they play in my life. I pray that you would continue to guide me on this journey and that you would help me to see and understand the different aspects of my faith and my faith journey. Remind me that this is a marathon and not a sprint, that I can and should take breaks when I need them, and that I am worthy of this hard work I am doing.

VIII

WHO ARE YOUR PEOPLE:
FINDING YOUR CIRCLE

I had barely stepped off the treadmill when the phone rang, and Missy's face lit up my phone screen.

"Nobody's dead," she said as soon as I answered. We've had so many tragedies in our collective lives over the past several years that we've resorted to greeting one another with that reassurance whenever we call each other.

"Okay, good! What's up?" I responded because Missy knows I hate talking on the phone and firmly believe in the "that could have been a text" philosophy.

"I think I need your help today, after all. This is a disaster, and I just want to get this done today," she lamented from the other side of the phone.

"I'll be there in 15 minutes." I changed out of my running clothes into my work clothes that her husband, Brent, always said made me look like a homeless painter, grabbed a water bottle and yeti of coffee, and headed out the door. I didn't see the point in showering, considering I knew what I was getting ready to walk into.

Missy's father-in-law had passed away unexpectedly days earlier, and his house was in complete disarray. He suffered from a litany of health problems and Missy and her husband, Brent, had been working with the VA to get him a better and safer living arrangement. They never saw that fulfilled, though, as he passed away unexpectedly in his home, leaving his four dogs unattended for far too long and leaving the house in complete shambles.

Having already spent an entire day cleaning out the kitchen and one bathroom, I knew what I was in for. I pulled into the driveway and parked beside our five-ton dump trailer we had dropped off earlier in the week. Missy met me with Febreeze and trash bags as I walked in the back door. Both of our Type A personalities kicked in, and we chose a corner that would serve as our starting point as we worked our way through the house throwing away the trash, filling tubs for Goodwill, and keeping the things we felt were sentimental. We were created for this type of work.

A few minutes into our purge, I asked Missy where Brent was. She said he had gone to breakfast with Russ, and they'd be out to help after they were done eating. I knew Russ as one of Brent's lifelong friends who was part of the group chat Missy and I affectionately named "The Girls." It earned that title because during our weekend evenings together, Brent's phone dinged from that group chat more than Missy and mine combined.

I knew of Russ from school. My mom had been his fifth-grade teacher, and he had graduated with my brother. I also knew that he had been a senior when I was a lowly little freshman, and so the odds of him knowing who I was were slim at best. Additionally, Brent had been telling me for a solid year that when I was ready to date again, I should date Russ. I love Brent, but I wasn't sure about dating, period, and I feared what would happen if I dated Russ

WHO ARE YOUR PEOPLE

and it didn't work out. Consequently, I laughed it off and avoided Brent's persistence in the matter.

Over the next week, we finished cleaning everything out of the house, took the trailer to the dump, and hauled stuff to Goodwill. By the time the next weekend arrived, we were finally able to breathe again. We were sitting at Missy and Brent's eating pizza, telling stories, and laughing way too much when I realized Missy and Brent had never said anything else about the Russ situation.

Brent immediately started talking about how much fun he thought Russ and I would have together and how he wasn't about to give Russ my number until I asked him to, but Missy was strangely quiet. I remember where I was standing in her kitchen and how she looked at me with that earnest yet empathetic look when she finally chimed into the conversation: "Russ doesn't go to church, and I don't really know how he feels about Jesus," she said, "and I know that's important to you. So, I haven't said anything else to you about it because I know what your priorities are in a relationship, and I'm just not sure he's a good fit for your priorities and your needs."

Brent was speechless, and Brent was never speechless.

I paused before I responded, sitting in the love and gratitude I had for this woman God had placed in my life at birth, who knew me and loved me so well. She was right. I had spoken to those needs and priorities for five years, and compromise was not on the horizon for me.

"I need to process this and spend some time talking to God about all of this," I told them. Brent looked a little hurt, but he ultimately understood because he understood me, and Missy didn't bat an eye at my response.

After reading Joyce Meyer's *Battlefield of the Mind*, I started the habit of writing down my needs on index cards and taping them to my bathroom mirror. As God would answer my prayers, I would take the index card off my mirror. Those index cards served as reminders to talk to God about my needs and desires as well as a reminder of God's faithfulness in my life as I saw those empty spaces where index cards had been. I came home that night and wrote "Russ" on an index card and taped it to my mirror.

I journaled, talked to God, sought His wisdom and His desires for me, and ultimately ended up talking in depth with Missy about the entire situation. On the fifth day, after God had consistently been nudging me toward getting to know Russ, I wrote this giant note about where I was, what I was feeling, and how God was nudging me, and I sent it to Missy, who immediately called me (and told me no one had died).

It was the next day that Missy spoke with Russ for an hour, and it was the day after that when Brent passed along my number, and Russ texted me the first time. Two days later, we had our first date, and we've been inseparable since. The irony of the entire situation is that at the end of our first date, Russ brought up his faith. Missy had told him her concerns and my needs and priorities. As it turned out, he was also a survivor of severe church hurt and had been out of church for a decade because of his wounds, but he still loved Jesus and knew God. I knew after this conversation about faith and church hurt that Russ was one of my people. He understood where I was coming from and had empathy for all I had been through. I understood his pain with the church as well, though, in a way he had never experienced from others before.

I spent so many of my teen and adult years only surrounding myself with people who claimed Christ and, mostly, attended the same church or type of church as I did. My circle was so small and so closed-minded that it caused me to miss out on so much of life. While my current circle is still pretty small – by choice – it's lively, vibrant, loving, empathetic, and understanding. It's full of people like Missy, Brent, and Russ – who know me at the very deepest

WHO ARE YOUR PEOPLE

levels of my core and who love me anyway. We don't have masks, we don't portray fake Facebook-y lives, and we certainly don't hide our failures or weaknesses. We call each other when we need someone to wade through the piles of dog crap with us while we clean out horrendous houses, and we know each other well enough to be able to say, "This will feed your soul" or "This isn't for you."

These are my people.

FAITH, PHARISEES, AND FUN

My name is Kristen, and I was a teenage Pharisee.

Missy and I both grew up in similar church situations, being brainwashed to follow a very specific set of rules and only spend time with other Christians – because we were supposed to be in the world and not of the world and to view every person we came into contact with who was not a Christian as the mission field. It makes us both a little sick to look back on this time in our lives.

Do you want to know how I know God has a sense of humor? Missy and I both married our first husbands in our early 20s and were divorced from them in our 30s. Missy's second husband, Brent, went to school with me and graduated with my brother. We weren't friends in high school, and even though Brent sporadically attended the same church as me, he enjoyed his high school years a little differently than I did. My teenage Pharisee self would have judged the crap out of Brent and his life and only hung out with him if I thought I could have brought him around to Jesus.

After going through a traumatic divorce, being a single mom for three years, and leaving her life, job, house, and career to move back to her hometown, Missy worked through her own faith deconstruction and reconstruction, and she abandoned her life as a Pharisee. When she and Brent first started dating, we spent countless evenings laughing about the differences between Brent's high school days and ours, as well as laughing at ourselves for our sheltered and closed-minded high school days.

Then, we added Russ to our inner circle, and the stories became even more elaborate and the laughter even louder. I constantly just laugh and smile knowingly as I look at our circle. Here are Missy and I – the teenage Pharisees now married to Brent and Russ – the guys whose souls would have been on our prayer lists when we were in high school. And I can see God chuckling at the entire scene.

Here's the thing about our circle: even though we all attend church together, our lives and conversations are filled with all sorts of things – not just church, faith, Jesus, God, etc. Those topics come up, and we discuss them at length, but our relationships are not consumed with those topics. We have the freedom to allow the depth and breadth of who we are and what we love to dominate our lives and conversations without always feeling the need to connect it to God and the church. That's not something I ever had before my faith deconstruction and reconstruction because I was taught to overspiritualize everything.

For those of you who have spent your entire lives in high-control religion, fundamentalism, or evangelism, you might have noticed a pattern in your relationships where every single conversation has to circle back around to a Bible verse, a lesson from God, a Bible story or character, your faith, or the church in general. That's the way my life was for 38 years. I remember when one of my friends married a man who didn't go to church. I was so distraught because I legitimately didn't know what they were going to talk about. I didn't see what they could possibly have in common if he didn't go to church with her. I was completely unaware that I could have close relationships with people that did not revolve around church.

That was part of my conditioning that I struggled and struggled with breaking. It took me quite a while to be comfortable in my relationships with my closest friends and just relax, be authentic, be honest, and not feel like every single time we talked I had to point the conversation or the topic of our conversation back to my faith, our church, or God. I didn't realize that was a coping mechanism and, at times, a defense mechanism. I had to learn that this habit was keeping me from being honest about my feelings, my life, and my experiences. I didn't realize I could hang out with my friends and just have fun – that this was what healthy relationships looked like.

These healthy relationships are those relationships that allow you to be authentic, transparent, and honest and that accept you as your raw and real self. If I'm being 100% honest with you, then I have to admit that these relationships I immersed myself in for years in my faith community weren't healthy. They were built on masks and fake realities. Everyone feared honesty and weakness because they feared what others would think of them and what that would say about them spiritually. Consequently, my circles during those years were filled with fake people who spent more time judging others and pointing out their flaws to make themselves feel better about their lives than honesty and connection. The sad reality is that sometimes, the circles we find in our faith communities can be the absolute worst circles for us.

RELATIONSHIPS SHOULD SUPPORT YOUR RECONSTRUCTION PROCESS

It's so hard to walk away from any relationship that has sustained us in the past, but walking away from relationships in faith communities can be even more difficult because of the consequences of removing yourself from that circle. Your reconstruction should not prompt your friends to put you on the prayer list unless they are genuinely praying for your process and not your soul because they think you're a heretic who's going to hell. That can be a fine but important line in so many of our faith communities.

Friends who love you and genuinely care about you will pray for you and your process while also not being afraid to ask you genuine questions because they care about you and want to support you. Too often, though, in our faith communities, we're met with folks who ask us "searching" questions instead of genuine questions. They are more concerned with *searching out* how you're "failing" Christ according to their ideals than they are about the major life-changing work you're doing in your reconstruction. They ask you questions because they want to know your gossip more than they want to support you.

I wrote a devotional for Christmas a few years ago, and as I was preparing to write it, I was struck by the relationship between Mary, Jesus's mom, and Elizabeth, John the Baptist's mom. If you haven't read the Biblical account recently, you can find Luke's version of it in his first chapter. Here's what gets me about the relationship between these two women: the unconditional love and support in the face of absolutely bizarre circumstances. Elizabeth was too old to have children and found out she was pregnant with John. Meanwhile, Mary was this young, unwed teenager who found out from an angel she'd be birthing Jesus. While those details are strange enough, the part that hits me right in the feels is right after this.

As soon as Mary found out she was pregnant, she left and went to Elizabeth. She just left and took off from Nazareth to make the 90-mile journey to Ain Karim. Mary had a solid four or five days to soak in the news and figure out how to break it to Elizabeth while she made this trek. When she gets to Elizabeth, the cousins embrace and all kinds of holy heck breaks loose there.

At the moment her aunt heard Mary's voice, the baby within Elizabeth's womb jumped and kicked. And suddenly, Elizabeth was filled to overflowing with the Holy Spirit![44]

John leapt in Elizabeth's womb, and the Holy Spirit entered Elizabeth, spurring her prophecy, which was followed by Mary's heartfelt prayer.

While this is a fantastic reunion between the two women, I can't help but read between the lines of the interaction. Maybe I'm just too much of a skeptic, but if my teenage cousin showed up at my house and told me she was pregnant by the Holy Spirit and carrying the savior of the world in her womb, I'd have questions. Elizabeth doesn't, though. The only thing she feels at Mary's arrival and news is overwhelming joy and support.

God was clearly in that friendship and that reunion, and I believe God can work the same kinds of miracles today for you and your relationships. I believe He is faithful and just, and He wants to give you a circle of people who will walk through your miraculous journey of reconstruction with you with the same overwhelming joy and support Mary and Elizabeth had for one another. These women were in terribly bizarre situations, situations that could have made others question them endlessly, but in each other, they found nothing other than support.

Your situation might not feel as miraculous or as odd as Elizabeth's or Mary's today, but you might find yourself facing the same kinds of skepticism and judgment from your faith community as Elizabeth and Mary undoubtedly found from others in theirs. Just like Elizabeth and Mary didn't have to face their seasons alone, my prayer is that you don't either, that God will send you your own Elizabeth or Mary to walk with you through it.

---

[44] Luke 1:41 TPT

KNOWING WHO IS NOT IN YOUR CIRCLE

Just as important as knowing who is in your circle, who your Marys and your Elizabeths are, it's equally important for you to know who *isn't* in your circle. This process is hard enough on its own, but when you're trying to walk through this with people who are not supporting you or your journey, it makes it even more difficult. The sad reality is that there are church people out there who seem genuinely interested in you and concerned about your journey, but, in truth, their motive is to gain fodder about you for them to gossip about.

That is a hard situation for multiple reasons. First, it's always difficult to find out that people you thought loved you and supported you only love you and support you when you think the same as them. But, secondly, it can be difficult to be the subject of gossip within the very circles you were once an integral part of. I don't think it ever gets easier to be the subject of gossip; however, I learned a valuable lesson about dealing with this type of situation when I read Lysa Tuerkeurst's *It's Not Supposed to be This Way*. Lysa talks about the difference between news and truth. She says:

> News comes to tell us what we are dealing with.
>
> Truth comes from God and then helps us process all we are dealing with.
>
> News and truth aren't always one and the same.[45]

It might very well be news that you are in a season of deconstruction and reconstruction, just like it might be news that the people who were once in your circle now see you as a prodigal, a heretic, or a lost sheep. That's all it is, though: news. It's not the truth. The truth is what comes from God and helps us deal with

---

[45] TerKeurst, Lysa. *It's Not Supposed to Be This Way.* Nelson Books, an Imprint of Thomas Nelson, 2018.

our deconstruction/reconstruction process at the same time as we learn to deal with these people and our former circles.

Our truth is that we aren't heretics, prodigals, or lost sheep. We are people who desperately want to be closer to God and a little more like Jesus, and we are feeling our way, sometimes in the dark, along the path to get to that point. How others see us on this journey is not our truth; it's simply their news.

When I think about these circles, the judgment, and the gossip, I always think of Jesus and his relationship with the Pharisees, who were always trying to trick and trap him. Even though they belonged to the same religious group and faith communities, they weren't on the same page or even in the same book, it seemed, most of the time. They were so focused on the law that they couldn't see the man standing before them and the good he was doing.

That might be true for you, too. You might find yourself in a circle or a faith community where the others are so focused on the rules, performance, law, moral obligations, and masks that they can't see you for the human you are standing right in front of them doing good, hard, worthy work. Just like the Pharisees were not Jesus's people or his circle, these people and communities are not part of your circle, and they are not your people.

We can read about the interactions between Jesus and the Pharisees and see they didn't have his best interests at heart, but we can go a step further and realize they didn't have the best interests of their people at heart either. Luke explains in chapter 6:

> On another Sabbath, Jesus was teaching in the synagogue. In the room with him was a man with a deformed right hand. Everyone watched Jesus closely, especially the Jewish religious leaders and the religious scholars, to see if Jesus would heal on a Sabbath, for they were eager to find a reason to accuse him of breaking the Jewish laws.

Jesus, knowing their every thought, said to the man with the deformed hand, "Come and stand here in the middle of the room." So he got up and came forward.

Jesus said to all who were there, "Let me ask you a question. Which is better: to heal or to do harm on the Sabbath? I have come to save a life, but you have come to find a life to destroy."[46]

The Pharisees were more concerned with the law and how Jesus might break it than they were about healing, and that is happening too often to many of us today as well. We have people in our faith communities or former faith communities who were once part of our inner circles but who now don't have our best interests at heart. They care about our church attendance and our belief in their system more than they care about our healing.

That realization was one of the worst for me as I was deconstructing/reconstructing. I lost many people who had spent their entire lives preaching to me about the importance of love. As soon as I started to think a little differently, though, I was no longer worthy of their love. That was traumatic, and it required me to heal and grieve the relationships I had lost.

GRIEVING THE LOSS OF RELATIONSHIPS

I saw a meme the other day that said something to the effect of "Just because we don't go to the same church anymore doesn't mean we can't be friends." I liked it and shared it immediately because it should be true. Too often, it isn't. The only people I'm friends with from the church I grew up in are those people who got blackballed and left, and my parents are the same way. In some ways, I think it must be worse for them. They spent years in rela-

---

[46] Luke 6:6-9 TPT

tionships with these people. They raised their children together. They spent weekends together. They had a community in small groups with these people. As soon as we left, though, the lines of communication were severed.

That is a loss, and it has to be grieved like a loss. In a sense, the loss of these relationships is as bad as death, and they have to be treated that way. If you're like me, then the time you spent in those religious communities taught you not to feel your feelings, but I'm here to tell you today that the best thing you can do to heal is to acknowledge those feelings and to grieve the friendships that you lost so that you can work toward healing.

Betrayal is never easy in relationships. It doesn't matter what form it takes; there is always a sting that comes with it. I spent my entire life hearing about Judas's betrayal of Jesus, but I don't know that I ever heard anyone discuss the emotional toll that it took on Christ. John mentions this in chapter 13 verse 21. He says:

> Then Jesus was moved deeply in his spirit. Looking at his disciples, he announced, "I tell you the truth—one of you is about to betray me.[47]"

Jesus was having His last supper here on earth with his disciples – the friends He had spent three years intimately in ministry with–and He knew one of those friends was going to betray Him, turn His back on Him, and sell Him out. And Jesus was heartbroken by it. That one sentence, "Then Jesus was moved deeply in his spirit" means that Jesus felt a profound tenderness in His spirit moving Him deeply. Have you ever thought about that scene in this way? I know I hadn't. When I thought about the humanity of Christ here, how He was deeply distraught by the betrayal of His friend, it changed my entire perception of this relationship.

---

[47] John 13:21 TPT

I quit being angry with Judas for being the villain, and I started feeling empathy for the heartbroken Jesus – the man who was watching as one of His closest friends walked away and turned against Him. I know I've questioned how so many people who claimed Christ could turn their backs on me, but sometimes I forget that Judas didn't just claim Christ; he walked beside him, ministered with Him, and healed with Him, and yet, he still turned his back on his friend.

Frankly, it sucked. It was heartbreaking for Jesus. He felt that betrayal in His soul. So, why should we be any different? We don't have to handle these betrayals and heartbreaks with strength and without caring. We can be heartbroken by them. We can recognize that they suck and acknowledge and sit in those feelings – just like Jesus did.

FINDING YOUR CIRCLE

In addition to grieving those lost relationships, there's one more thing I would encourage you to do. It's easy to get caught up in the negative and to be overwhelmed by what and who you've lost. I would encourage you to look around and recognize the people who are still there, too. Who is still sitting at the table with you?

I've been so fortunate to have Missy, Brent, and Russ in my circle, even if Russ did come into it after my deconstruction phase. They have consistently sat at the table with me, loved me through my journey, listened to me rant, asked questions, and prayed for me through this season. They aren't the only people in my circle, though. There are people I've been in ministry with – before, during, and after my deconstruction/reconstruction – who have faithfully loved and encouraged me in this hard work. Those are my people. That is my circle.

If you are struggling to find your circle, let me encourage you to not rule out the virtual world. I have met so many people through social media who are trudging through this journey, too, who are seeking community and connection, and who I view as compatriots in this battle. I look forward to reading their thoughts on their posts, interacting with them in comments, and feeling a sense of belonging and understanding with them.

You might not have a circle that understands you and what you're going through in your neighborhood, but you can absolutely find community online. There are many others out there struggling with the same questions, grappling with the same theology, and desperately trying to find like-minded people. Those might be the people you need right now, and that's okay. Maybe you aren't ready to lay your reconstruction out for everyone to see right now. I get it. It's a process. But don't sit in this alone. Don't close off your circle because of fear. Find people who get you and get this, and connect with them.

Lastly, friends, let me remind you that your circle does not have to revolve around your faith and theology to be your circle. You can go out with your friends and talk about your kids, work, hobbies, the books you're reading, and the senseless TV you're watching without talking about church and theology. In fact, you should probably do that more often. Take a break from this weighty worthy work to live your life and have freedom from rehashing your church hurt, spiritual abuse, and religious trauma. You deserve it, and you owe that to yourself.

REFLECTIONS: WHO ARE YOUR PEOPLE

Remember:

- Your circle should be filled with people who support you in your reconstruction.
- You don't have to talk about church, theology, and Bible verses in every conversation you have.
- The people who put you on the prayer list and call you a heretic are not your circle.
- Deconstructing/Reconstructing will inevitably cause you to lose people who were once in your circle.
- You can have circles outside of your faith community.
- Find yourself your Mary/Elizabeth.

Receive:

Luke 1:39-45 TPT:

Afterward, Mary arose and hurried off to the hill country of Judea, to the village where Zechariah and Elizabeth lived. 40 Arriving at their home, Mary entered the house and greeted Elizabeth. 41 At the moment her aunt heard Mary's voice, the baby within Elizabeth's womb jumped and kicked. And suddenly, Elizabeth was filled to overflowing with the Holy Spirit! 42 With a loud voice she *prophesied with power*:

> "Mary! You are a woman given the highest favor
> and privilege above all others,
> for your child is destined to bring God great delight.
> 43 How did I deserve such a remarkable honor
> to have the mother of my Lord come and visit me?
> 44 The moment you came in the door and greeted me,
> my baby danced inside me with joy!
> 45 Great favor rests upon you, for you have believed
> every word spoken to you from the Lord."

Reflect:

1. Who are the people you spend the most time with?
2. Who do you turn to when you need to tell the truth?
3. How do those people respond to your truth and your reconstruction?
4. Who are the people who you need to have boundaries with during this reconstruction process?
5. What relationships are you mourning since you began deconstructing/reconstructing?
6. What online resources are you utilizing to build your circle?

Prayer:

God, thank you for the people who have supported me and stood in my corner throughout my reconstruction process. God, I pray that you would continue to show me the people who are meant to be part of my circle, as well as those who should not have access to me during this time. I pray you help heal my wounds and my heart as I recover from the people and relationships I've lost during this time. Help me to continue to be hopeful and healing to others as they embark on their own deconstruction/reconstruction journeys.

IX

COMMUNITY:
FITTING IN AFTER
DECONSTRUCTION AND
RECONSTRUCTION

I listened as the surgical nurse gave my dad his instructions after having multiple stents placed in his heart. Nothing really piqued my interest until I heard the nurse say, "And no driving for a week." I immediately looked at my dad quizzically, silently asking him if he knew he didn't have driving privileges for the week. He stared back at me with the same confusion I was feeling.

When we were finally able to leave the hospital several hours later, I pulled the truck around, waited for him to get in, and then asked if he knew about the driving restrictions. "Nope, this is the first I've heard of it," he told me. "Guess you're going to have to take us to church Sunday," he said in some weird combination of humor, questioning, and apology.

See, I try to be a good daughter and guest when I visit my parents and their snowbird existence down South. The one "good daughter and guest" thing I just can't do is go to their church. More on that later. They have been snowbirds for a decade, splitting their time between the Midwest and the South but still calling the Midwest home. They kept their roots here while their hearts were constantly in the south. Because they were founding members of our church and I've been the mouthpiece for them to all of our family members, I spent an inordinate amount of time at church and via text answering the recurring question: "When are your parents coming home?"

My answer has always been the same: "Your guess is as good as mine. I'm always the last to know." Which is God's honest truth. My dad is one of those folks who consistently has a plan brewing in his mind, but he's not the greatest at sharing that plan with others – especially those he's closest to (read: me). The irony of this situation is that they live in the mother-in-law suite connected to our house. You would think if anyone should know when they're "coming home," it should be me. But, after years of this, I've simply come to expect to be the last to know.

At this point, I think he just does this stuff for sport, and I think he kind of likes the element of surprise and reaction he and my mom receive when they walk into our church after an extended absence. My mom is a social butterfly who flits around the warehouse, smiling and chatting with everyone – whether she knows them or not– while my dad sits in his assigned seat in the back of the warehouse and lets everyone come to him.

The last time they were home, he commented about how many new faces were around and how he didn't feel like he knew very many people anymore. I explained to him how I had just had this revelation about not knowing many people myself. When Jody and I took the reins of women's ministry, completely rebranded it, and essentially started it over, we stood at the doors of the warehouse for a couple of Sundays to make contact with the women in our church and to give them the information for the survey we had created. I realized very quickly that of the hundreds of people who attended our church, I knew about 50 of them. I can't tell you how many people attend our church because we refuse to count or to have formal membership nonsense. I know we have around 400 chairs set up, and most of them are full. That's the best I can tell you.

He talked about how it's so weird that he's been there since day one, and now people probably think he's just another visitor. My parents weren't just there from day one; they were integral parts of making our church what it is today. It was my dad who sat in that room with the other pastors who had been kicked out, fired, or removed from their churches and talked about how we had to do church differently. He was the one who looked those pastors in the eyes and explained how the camaraderie and brotherhood that happens in the local dive bars is the same kind of camaraderie and brotherhood we should have in the church.

This was the early 2000s during the boom of megachurches. They visited those megachurches. They read the literature. And then they respectfully put it down and followed their hearts, their experiences, and the constant guiding of the Holy Spirit to create something so different the local churches and faith communities didn't even know what to do with it. We were called all sorts of things by local faith leaders and churches – all of which implied we were heretics.

These other churches struggled with the fact that instead of joining in with a local church's protest of the neighboring strip club, we took cookies to the strippers. They didn't like that our music was loud. They scoffed at the fact that we didn't make people take their hats off. And they really couldn't understand how we didn't pass the offering plate but just had some baskets at the back of the church by the doors – until someone helped themselves to the cash. Then, we had to attach locked boxes to the wall. But, still. They wanted to know how many "members" we had and what our attendance was on a typical Sunday morning. We didn't know. They didn't like that either. They questioned everything we did.

Nothing we did was "right" in their eyes. But, it wasn't their eyes we were concerned with. Soon, our seats filled up with the misfits, the misunderstood, and the marginalized. We offered a safe space for all sorts of folks who never found church to be a safe place before–the formerly incarcerated, the survivors of church hurt, the defected Catholics, the divorced, the "prodigals" who weren't welcomed back to their former faith communities with the open arms so clearly apparent in the parable.

There are two major churches within spitting distance of our church. We know that our flavor of church is not for everyone. It's not uncommon to hear Jeff say through the mic from the stage on any given Sunday that if we are not for you, we can help you find a church that is. Soon, though, something strange started to happen in our community at these other churches. When people would show up at these other area churches needing help, those churches wouldn't help them, but they would always send them to us. So often people would show up on our doorstep or contact us through Facebook Messenger, telling us another church had sent them to us, that it became laughable. Here were these people desperate for help, and the same people who had been vocally and openly criticizing us were sending the least of these to our doorstep because they knew we would feed them, clothe them, love them, and treat them like Jesus treated people and told us to treat people.

I am incredibly fortunate to have this church community, to have been there from before day one, and to know that I am in a safe place for reconstruction within our church community, but I know not everyone is as fortunate as I am. For so many of us in this reconstruction space and on this reconstruction journey, we can feel at a complete loss when it comes to finding community. So, what do you do as a reconstructing person of faith trying to find a church?

WHEN YOU WANT TO GO TO CHURCH

One of the hardest parts of the faith deconstruction and reconstruction process can be leaving a faith community that was an integral part of your life. I've learned, too, that one of the most anxiety-inducing stops on this journey can be when you feel that nudge to get back into a church or faith community. I'm not a mental health professional, so I'm saying this as a complete layperson with no expertise except my own experience. Church, for those of us on the other side of deconstruction, can feel an awful lot like having a PTSD episode. I love my church and am comfortable in the community, but there have still been times, even in the last year, when I've found my heart rate increasing and the cold sweat starting in the middle of a service because of a topic that is being addressed, not because the Holy Spirit was moving, but because something that was said sounded too familiar to something traumatic from my past church experiences.

This is not easy work, friend.

For so many people on this side of deconstruction and working through the reconstruction process, the task of finding a church/faith community can feel daunting and nearly impossible. The biggest hurdle for many people is knowing where to even start. The good news is that if you've made it this far, you have a strong handle on what your priorities are for your faith, what your triggers are, and what the basic tenets of your faith are. That is the perfect starting point for your quest for a new church/faith community.

We are fortunate to live in an era where we have access to so much information right at our fingertips. When you first start this process of finding a church, utilize your resources. Before I ever visit a church, I stalk them online. You can learn so much from a church's online presence. You can find out how they feel about technology, what their core beliefs are, and what other people are saying about them, and you can even watch services from most churches right on their Facebook pages or YouTube channels.

I've spent hours looking for a church local to my parents that I can comfortably attend when I visit. I've stalked countless churches online, attempting to find one that aligns with my belief system and needs. I'd love to share my process with you and hope you can find a way to use it and adapt it to your needs.

When I first open a Facebook profile or website for a church, there are a few things I look for immediately that might not matter to you but that are giant red flags for me:

- Is there a scoreboard in clear view that shows the attendance, offerings, etc?
- What are the people on stage wearing? Does appearance seem to be more important than worship?
- Does the decor and stage setup scream "old school traditional" or even "90s contemporary"?

These might sound petty or even stereotypical to some, but I've learned over the years that I can infer a ton of things from simply seeing a picture from a service.

If a church passes the visual test, then I start digging deeper into their website. Most websites will have a page dedicated to their core beliefs. This is always my second step. Before I even think about walking through the doors of a church, I want to know what they believe. Maybe that visual test isn't important to you and your faith priorities, but the core beliefs certainly should be. You know what your core beliefs are at this point, and when you are looking for a church, those core beliefs should be at the forefront of your mind. If you read through this list on their website and you find it's full of red flags and triggers for you, then you will know immediately that you should close that website and move on to a different church.

If I make it past the core belief page without twitching and wanting to bang my head against a wall, I visit the staff/leadership page to see who they are paying and who is guiding their work. For me, if I don't see any women on staff or in leadership, that's a huge red flag. But that's important to me. That might not be an issue for you. Each of us has to determine what we care about and what our priorities are in terms of the staff and leadership of a church.

Our church has four pastors, and they all have full-time jobs outside of ministry. Three of them share the preaching duties, and the fourth is solely the children's minister. Each pastor has their niche within the church as well. One of them is in charge of the teen ministry, one is the worship pastor, and the other focuses on hospital/funeral needs. I realize this is a different church model than most churches have, but it's a model that's important to me. Unfortunately, there don't seem to be many churches out there operating under this model. While this is an ideal for me, it's not a complete deal-breaker.

If I make it beyond the staff/leadership page, it's only then that I'll take the time to watch a service or two. Here's what I've learned–websites and Facebook pages can say anything, but the service itself ultimately tells me if the beliefs listed on a website truly align with what is happening in a church/faith community. I have seen countless churches have signs in their front yards that read "All are welcome here," but whose core beliefs and reality are more aligned to "All are welcome here as long as they share the exact same belief system as we do." The only way to cut through the lip service is to watch a Sunday service.

After I've watched a few services, if there still are no glaring red flags, I'll give myself a pep talk and go to visit. As an introvert in a new environment, and as someone who has survived severe church hurt and religious trauma, I prefer to sit in the back and observe without any interaction, if possible. Now, not everyone is going to share my need for solitude and observation, and I understand that. I don't mind if people talk to me, but I draw a hard line at the "stand up and greet your neighbor" crowd.

Those are my preferences, though, and I know we all have different needs. Identifying your needs and figuring out what makes you comfortable is what's most important in this quest to find a church. The reality is that it might take you some time to figure out what that looks like, and that's completely okay. There's no time limit on how long it should take you to find a church, and there's no limit to how many churches you can visit.

As you attempt to find a church that feels like home to you and as you visit more churches, you'll figure out what's important to you in a faith community, and part of that process is figuring out what you can agree to disagree on and what you absolutely will not compromise on. Only you can know what those things are. If you find yourself in a church/faith community that makes you uncomfortable or that is preaching something that goes against your core values, here's the beauty of the world we live in: you can leave.

Let me say that a little louder for those in the back: you don't have to sit through a church service that makes you uncomfortable. They cannot hold you hostage. You can absolutely get up in the middle of the service and make your exit. That's one of the reasons why I choose to sit in the back of a church and at the end of an aisle. I can make an easy exit if I need to.

You should never feel guilty for this choice to leave. No one knows what your history is. They don't know the church hurt, spiritual abuse, or religious trauma you've endured in the past, and they definitely haven't been walking along with you on this tedious and difficult journey of faith deconstruction and reconstruction. You've done the hard work up until this point, and you can continue to do the hard work even if that hard work looks like walking out of a church service. For so many of us who lived through high-control religion, this is not a freedom we ever had in our lives. For some of you, the thought of walking out in the middle of a service is causing you to have severe anxiety right now. I get it. I see you.

Let me tell you one thing I've learned about exiting a church that was not aligned with my beliefs during this process – it is freeing. The most powerful I've ever felt in life was when I removed myself from a faith community that was triggering and didn't align with my own beliefs. That was the moment I realized I finally had agency over my faith and the faith communities I would choose to be part of.

The sad reality is that you might find yourself walking out of countless church services as you search for a church/faith community. That can be disheartening and completely depressing. It can make you feel like you will never find a physical church to call home. While this is a terrible feeling, and it is a horrible place to find yourself in, the good news is that there are other options.

THE HOME CHURCH

There were no megachurches as we know them during Jesus's time on earth. Those were created by man, and while I think they probably have a place and meet the needs of certain people, they don't meet the needs of everyone. Even the smaller community churches we still have, and that are most like the synagogues of Jesus's day, they meet the needs of some, but they don't and can't meet the needs of everyone. So, what does that leave us with? In our quests for a church home, we often overlook the home church.

For those of us coming from high-control religion, fundamentalism, or even evangelical backgrounds, it can be incredibly difficult to retrain our brains to think about church differently.

Many of us have probably been part of small groups or life groups or whatever your church called them, but we struggle with the idea that a group meeting in our home or a friend's home can be church.

Here's the thing, though: some of my best "church" moments have been in the comfort of my living room, surrounded by like-minded folks studying, thinking through, and discussing scripture, books, and ideas together. That community I've built in small spaces with a few people is a different kind of community than those that I've built in the bigger collective church as a whole.

Maybe a home church is a better option for you right now. As you learn to breathe again, a smaller, close-knit group of people with whom you read, discuss, and question is a healthier, and possibly even holier, space for you right now. If the thought of opening up your home scares you, then go somewhere else – like a coffee shop, a bookstore, or even the local library.

If you don't know where to start to find your people, look in local Facebook groups, check out threads and Instagram, and look at the community bulletin boards. I think you'll be pleasantly surprised that there are more people like you out there in your community than you ever knew before, and they are desperate for church and community as well.

VIRTUAL COMMUNITIES

If the thought of walking into a physical church building is still too much for you, I get it. If you aren't quite at a point where you feel comfortable sitting down in a home, coffee shop, etc., with others, then there are still other great opportunities to build community virtually.

I've never been a huge fan of social media for a variety of reasons. I prefer to have real-life friendships instead of virtual friendships, which I realize says entirely too much about my age and generation. But, I also find my heart breaking for the lives so many people attempt to portray online. I think it's getting better, but there are still times I scroll through my Facebook feed only to see the same people posting the same shiny, happy photos online while living a real life of misery. I just don't know what to do as a bystander to help these people.

You can imagine the shock and irony of the fact that a large part of my reconstruction community is a virtual community. When I started writing full-time and accepted the reality that I was a Christian Content Creator, whether I liked the title, the inferences, or the stereotypes, I began consistently creating content for all of these platforms. I guess I should say I tried creating content for these platforms for a hot minute. It took me a second to even figure out who I was creating content for and what that content should look like. After all, I'm a writer. I just wanted to write. I didn't want to create social media content, and I had no clue how to create social media content. It was a bit of a conundrum for me, to be completely honest.

In the process of trying to hone my niche and figure out how to create content, something really cool happened. I stumbled on so many like-minded folks online who I had no idea existed, and I started following and interacting with them. Something amazing happened to me: I realized I wasn't alone, that I wasn't the only person having these thoughts, and that many of my experiences with church hurt, spiritual abuse, and religious trauma were experiences other people shared.

As I followed more people and read more posts, I found myself saying, "Me too!" over and over again while gaining clarity about the damage done by the different aspects of the harmful theology I was raised in. Every day, I had multiple "aha" moments while finding compatriots to commiserate with.

It felt good.

As I continued to follow more people, read more amazing content, and engage with these individuals, I realized I had no idea I even needed this validation from this community of folks who were like me. It didn't take me long to realize how many amazing experts there are out there offering their wisdom through social media, podcasts, and Substacks. Before I knew it, I stumbled on experts in every damaged area I had from my church upbringing. I found amazing researchers studying the effects of purity culture, the misunderstanding of gender roles, the dangers of complementarian marriages, the long-term effects of high-control religion, and the responsibility placed on women for male thoughts and actions.

I found validation through those experts.

Another place where I found acceptance and camaraderie was Facebook Groups. While following individual accounts is great, participating in groups where you can be an active member and formulate bonds can be amazing for building community as well.

With groups, though, you do have to be a little more careful. Not all Facebook Groups are created equally. Some are just landing pages for people to sell you something. Others are full of spam, and still others are full of people who aren't committed to the process of reconstruction and want to spend all their time bashing Christians and Evangelicals.

Those can be hard places and damaging environments. Feel those groups out before you begin actively participating and getting immersed and involved in them. Once you know they're safe and they share the same values as you do, you can begin engaging and, hopefully, connect with another virtual community of survivors of church hurt, religious trauma, and spiritual abuse who are reconstructing or who have already reconstructed.

BEYOND FAITH COMMUNITIES

There is still one group of people we haven't talked to or about yet, and that's those of you who aren't ready for engagement with any type of faith community yet and might never be in a space where that's an option for you again. If you find yourself in that group, take heart, friend. You are not alone, and nothing is wrong with you. Healing takes time, and everyone heals differently.

For those of you in that category, and even those of you who are seeking faith communities, I want to give you an idea I would have found both radical and abhorrent when I was growing up: look beyond the church and your faith for community. Even though we are the most connected virtually a generation has ever been, research has shown that we are the loneliest we've ever been.

We all need community.

One of the most freeing things for me in my reconstruction journey has been abandoning the idea that I have to have all the answers and that the only people I can be in an intimate community with are those who share my belief system in terms of my faith. It took me years to break that mindset and to understand that I can have close connections to people who don't think like me or believe in the same God as me.

It took me years to understand that building community is so much more about sharing life with those who love and respect each other and their differences, who have some things in common but not necessarily everything in common, and who might be searching for themselves but who are, more importantly, open and accepting. Those are my people.

If you are finding yourself desperate for community, I want to encourage you to look beyond your faith at the other things you love. We are surrounded by groups for every type of interest. We have groups who bowl together weekly, run RC cars together, get together once a month to talk about books, share a new craft beer once a month, play trivia together on Tuesday nights, and sing Karaoke on the weekends. We have soccer leagues, pickleball leagues, and softball leagues that aren't connected to churches. We have coffee clubs, board game clubs, and golf leagues. The options really are endless.

Our in-person community options are extensive, and our virtual community options are essentially all-encompassing. But, they aren't just going to show up on our doorsteps; we have to actively look for them. And that's on us.

THE BREAKFAST CLUB

I started this chapter by explaining that I try to be a good daughter when I go to visit my snowbird parents. You might be wondering why I would need to find a good church to attend when I'm there since my dad has been such an integral part of my church at home.

When my folks first started snowbirding, they attended a church similar to our home church. After a year, they sold their snowbird house and moved 30 miles away. They drove 45 minutes on Sundays to attend that church for another several years. As they got a little older, the 45-minute drive got to be a bit much for them every Sunday, and they began to look for a church closer to them.

There happens to be a pretty large church a mile from their house that has two services on Sunday mornings. They began attending the early service with the rest of the 70 & up crowd. They sit in the same place and talk to the two other couples around them every Sunday. It works for them at this point in their lives, regardless of all the questions I ask about this choice.

I tried to go a few times, but I ended up walking out of each service much more outraged than I went in every single time. It reminds me too much of my childhood. It triggers me repeatedly, and I have boundaries now. So, I don't go. And my dad respects that. He typically comes home on the Sundays I'm there and says, "It's probably a good thing you weren't there today..." and then he proceeds to tell me the appalling things that were said from the stage.

What's funny to me is that he knows they're appalling. He knows why I would be triggered by them. But, he stays. Even though I don't get it, I respect that it's his choice and that his needs for a church/faith community are different from my own. I don't try to get him to go anywhere else (anymore), and he doesn't try to convince me to go there. Hence the reason why I keep trying to find a church to go to when I visit them.

My dad is a thoughtful and insightful man. I know his experience of getting blackballed from a church affected him greatly, even though he doesn't talk about it. I know his vision for what church should be like came from his own experiences as a teenager, not even old enough to have a license, going to the bar to pick his dad up. I know his heart. Even though the church he attends works for him, I know it will never work for me. I also know, though, that the church he attends is not where he has found his community. You might find yourself in the same position as my parents.

I've watched as both of my parents have created a community outside of their church, and it makes me so proud. For two people who were brainwashed for 40-plus years by high-control religion and legalism to be able to walk away from that and meet Jesus, it is utterly miraculous. To see them flourishing now in their little breakfast club makes me feel like a proud "parent."

There's a little dive in their town called Grannies. They've loved the place since they began snowbirding. As they spent more time south, they went there more and more frequently, and earlier and earlier. Soon, they were going to Grannies for breakfast six days a week as soon as they opened. I noticed my dad mentioning more and more folks from their breakfasts on a regular basis.

And before I knew it, my parents were going to dinner with them, helping out on their home projects, and participating in group text messages.

These are their people. This is their community–a group of retired folks who just happened to eat at the same place for breakfast every day. The staff knows them all by name, what time they each arrive daily, and where their assigned seats in the restaurant's backroom are. And now, the staff has bought each of them coffee mugs with their names on them.

It is a strong, rich, healthy, and beautiful community.

If you don't feel comfortable in a church, a home church isn't for you, and you are desperate for connection and community, you find yourself your own Breakfast Club, friends.

REFLECTIONS: COMMUNITY

Remember:

- Only you know your core beliefs.
- When you want to go to church, utilize your resources.
- You always have the freedom to leave a church/faith community.
- Home church is still a church.
- Seek virtual connections with discernment.
- Community exists outside of faith communities.
- Find your Breakfast Club.

Receive:

Proverbs 17:17 NIV:
A friend loves at all times.

Matthew 18:20 NIV:
For where two or more are gathered in my name, I am there.

Romans 12:16 NIV:
Live in harmony with one another.

Ephesians 4:2 NIV:
With tender humility and quiet patience, always demonstrate gentleness and generous love toward one another, especially toward those who may try your patience.

Reflect:

1. If you are looking for a church/faith community, what are your needs?

2. What are the issues you cannot "agree to disagree on" in church/faith communities?

3. What are the red flags for you when you are researching a church to attend?

4. If you are looking for a church or faith community, start today by researching churches in your area. What three do you want to examine in more depth?

5. What interests do you have outside of your faith?

6. How can you tap into those interests to find a community beyond a faith community?

Prayer:

God, thank you for bringing me to this place on my reconstruction journey. Thank you for allowing me to understand what my needs are for a church, and for the areas I'm still not sure about, I pray for clarity. Help me to understand myself and my faith better every day. I pray for the strength I need to seek out community, and I pray that you would help me guide me to those communities that are a good fit for me. If there are communities I need to stay away from, please allow me to discern that quickly. God, I know that I can find community outside of the church, and I pray you would help me to see those places and opportunities and to remember that those can be my people, too.

CONCLUSION:
TAKING ONE BREATH AT A TIME

It was just an average Sunday morning. I was sitting in my assigned seat in the next-to-last row of my section with my coffee in one hand and my notepad in the other. Missy and Brent were in the row in front of me, and the kids had just been dismissed to go to their classes. I settled into the message that was part of a series on Bible Stories Reconsidered. The series had been compelling so far, my favorite being the message that analyzed Samson's character because *oof*. That's a whole lot to unpack, and it reads very differently than the Sunday School version that's edited for the Kids's Bible.

I was excited as I saw the topic of the day was Esther. While I have many questions about the majority of this story, I have the utmost respect for the character of Esther, her wisdom at such a young age, her ability to strategize, and her willingness to sacrifice herself for her people. You can imagine my shock when the message somehow managed to paint Esther as a villain who never sought God's will in her life.

One of my tragic traits is my inability to hide my thoughts. They show all over my face and by the tilt of my head. And this was no different. Within just a few minutes of the message, I could feel my eyes squinting slightly, my lips pursing, and my head tilting. I wasn't verbally questioning, but my body language was screaming, "What the heck are you even talking about?" Before I knew it, I saw Missy pull out her phone and start typing, and within a few seconds my phone lit up with her text: "What the heck is this?" I quickly pecked out an expletive-laden (Forgive me, Jesus) response and hit send.

As the sermon continued, I felt my heart rate increase, the cold sweats started, and my fight-or-flight instinct went into overdrive. I was triggered, to say the least. I wasn't merely furious with this description of Esther; I was completely transported back to my childhood days of hearing sermon after sermon demeaning the heroic women of the Bible and telling me all the ways I was inferior to man.

When the service was over, I couldn't get out of there quickly enough. I had to take the afternoon to remind myself what is true, to breathe again, and to remember that this was not the church I grew up in, and everyone deserves a little grace for one bad sermon. Throughout the afternoon, Missy and I analyzed all the errors and faulty logic of the entire sermon, and by the evening, I had recovered. I was able to recover because I know the heart of the man who preached that sermon. I know his intent wasn't to demean women. His intent was to focus on God and allow His guidance in our lives. I could accept that his description of Esther was a bit superficial because I knew it wasn't meant as an attack on women in general.

But, man. It was a rough one. It feels like every time I think I have my reactions under control, some other issue related to my early church experiences and faulty theology rears its head, and I'm forced to face it head-on. Thankfully, I have the tools to do that now. I still get triggered, I still get exceptionally angry, and I still get frustrated, but I can feel those emotions and work through why I'm feeling them. I can sit in church on a Sunday morning and not feel like I'm holding my breath all the time, and that is a fantastically freeing feeling.

THIS IS A MARATHON, NOT A SPRINT.

I spent years as a runner. I read articles, researched the experts, and had all of the information I needed to know how to breathe correctly when I was running, but I could never do it. I even resorted to saying the mantra "in through the nose, out through the mouth" in my mind as I was running, but it never worked for me. I could never get my breathing under control, and I don't know if I can blame that for why I was never a great runner, but it certainly feels like an excellent excuse.

For the majority of my life, my faith felt the same in so many ways. No matter how hard I tried to follow the rules and check off the boxes, the weight wouldn't lift off my chest. I would sit in church or listen to people talk about their faith, and I would feel like I couldn't take a complete breath. I constantly felt like I had to be more and do more so that God would love me, bless me, and save me.

It was only throughout my deconstruction and reconstruction journey that I felt that weight lifting off my chest and finally realized I could breathe freely again, or maybe for the first time in my life. But it didn't happen quickly, and it definitely didn't happen overnight. It was like I was running that marathon I had always dreamed of running but could never quite make it to.

That marathon has taken me years, and I'm not sure I've even completed it yet, but I'm learning to breathe through it one breath and one day at a time. If there was a time limit on this marathon, I'd definitely be a DNF or Did Not Finish. Thankfully, there's no time limit on this. I still have questions that I don't have answers to, I still don't know why bad things happen to good people, I still don't understand the death and destruction in the Old Testament, and I still don't know if the unbelievable stories in the Bible are literal or mythical. Maybe as I continue breathing my way through this marathon, I'll figure some of those things out. But if I don't, that's okay too.

What I can breathe freely knowing along this journey and throughout this marathon, is the fact that I know who Jesus is and was, and that's where I choose to focus. I know Jesus spent His last hours with His friends, telling them to do it differently – to love God, but to love people too. I know that Jesus came to be grace with flesh on, and that He covers all my imperfections and my flaws, and I have plenty of those. But He covers everyone else's flaws and imperfections as well – even those people in those churches I run as far away from as I can.

This marathon has taught me to trust my gut. If something feels off about theology/tradition, I know to trust that feeling because that's usually how the Holy Spirit chooses to nudge me. Sometimes, that means I need to exit a situation. Sometimes, it means I need to do some more research, and sometimes it means I might need to assess what I'm doing or why the church is doing it. I know better than to excuse it or just blindly accept it as truth like I did for so many years.

LETTING GO AND BREATHING AGAIN

Friend, so much of this process has been about learning to lovingly let go of the past, to rediscover the present, and to have hope for the future. And we can't do any of those things if we're metaphorically holding our breath, closing our eyes, and wishing the hurt and the trauma away. We have to do the hard work, think critically, grieve our losses, and rebuild our faith one block at a time. My prayer is that you have started to do that throughout the course of reading about my journey. I hope that throughout these pages you have started to feel the weight lift off of your chest, and you can feel yourself beginning to breathe again, too– or maybe even for the first time.

This is still going to be a process; this journey will continue, and you'll still find yourself putting the finishing touches on your remodel and renovation. Remember that some days will be better than others, and some seasons will be easier than others. Regardless of the days and seasons, the only thing you can do is continue to take one breath at a time.

www.ingramcontent.com/pod-product-compliance
Lightning Source LLC
Chambersburg PA
CBHW021145130626
46554CB00005B/1665